1

# Table of Contents

# Introduction

The fact that you've purchased this book means two things. The first is that you're preparing for, or at least considering taking, the TABE exam, which can open new doors for your future by greatly expanding your options for careers. The second is that you've already taken an excellent first step in picking up this study guide.

We'll provide you with a detailed overview of the TABE, so that you know exactly what to expect on test day, then we'll cover all of the subjects over which you will be tested, providing multiple practice sections for you to test your knowledge and improve. Even if it's been a while since your last major examination, don't worry; we'll make sure you're more than ready!

## What is the TABE?

The TABE exam measures your skills through the high school level in Language Arts, Reading, and Mathematics. In short, it tests everything taught in high school, so employers and institutions will know that you are prepared for new training.

## Breaking Down the TABE

### Reading
- 50 questions, 50 minute time limit. Tests ability to read and interpret written passages.

### Mathematics
- There are 2 separate math sections on the TABE, however, for purposes of studying we will cover it in one chapter. While the presentation of questions is slightly different in each section, it really does not matter how the question is posed if you understand the fundamentals of math. It always comes down to adding, subtracting, multiplying, and dividing.
  - Math Comprehension: 40 questions, 25 minute time limit.
  - Math Application: 50 questions, 50 minute time limit.

### Language, Language Mechanics, Vocabulary, Spelling
- Tests knowledge of sentence structure, usage, mechanics, grammar, and organization. For purposes of this study guide, all sections are taught together. As you know, language, spelling, and vocabulary are all connected. Only the Language section is required; Language Mechanics, Vocabulary, and Spelling are optional.
  - Language: 55 questions, 55 minute time limit.
  - Language Mechanics (optional section): 20 questions, 14 minute time limit
  - Vocabulary (optional section): 20 questions, 15 minute time limit.
  - Spelling (optional section): 20 questions, 10 minute time limit.

## Scoring

There is no set passing or failing score on the TABE. You will need to check with the school or employment agency to find out what their minimum standards are. The scoring criteria is rather complicated, requiring a few different charts for each section. For many people, if you can get 70% of more of the question correct while working through this book, you should do fine.

**How This Book Works**

The subsequent chapters in this book are divided into a review of those topics covered on the exam. This is not to "teach" or "re-teach" you these concepts – there is no way to cram all of that material into one book! Instead, we are going to help you recall all of the information that you've already learned. Even more importantly, we'll show you how to apply that knowledge.

Each chapter includes an extensive review, with practice drills at the end to test your knowledge. With time, practice, and determination, you'll be completely prepared for test day.

# Chapter 1: The Reading Section

The Reading portion of the TABE will measure your ability to understand, analyze, and evaluate written passages. Tested passages will contain material from a variety of sources and on a number of different topics; after reading those passages, you will then have 50 minutes within which to answer 50 multiple-choice questions. Remember that the information in this section is applicable for other sections of the test! Reading, vocabulary, grammar, and spelling are all tied together in the English Language.

## The Main Idea

Finding and understanding the main idea of a text is an essential reading skill. When you look past the facts and information and get to the heart of what the writer is trying to say, that's the **main idea**. Imagine that you're at a friend's home for the evening:

> "Here," he says. "Let's watch this movie."

> "Sure," you reply. "What's it about?"

You'd like to know a little about what you'll be watching, but your question may not get you a satisfactory answer, because you've only asked about the subject of the film. The subject—what the movie is about—is only half the story. Think, for example, about all the alien invasion films ever been made. While these films may share the same general subject, what they have to say about the aliens or about humanity's theoretical response to invasion may be very different. Each film has different ideas it wants to convey about a subject, just as writers write because they have something they want to say about a particular subject. When you look beyond the facts and information to what the writer really wants to say about his or her subject, you're looking for the main idea.

One of the most common questions on reading comprehension exams is, "What is the main idea of this passage?" How would you answer this question for the paragraph below?

> "Wilma Rudolph, the crippled child who became an Olympic running champion, is an inspiration for us all. Born prematurely in 1940, Wilma spent her childhood battling illness, including measles, scarlet fever, chicken pox, pneumonia, and polio, a crippling disease which at that time had no cure. At the age of four, she was told she would never walk again. But Wilma and her family refused to give up. After years of special treatment and physical therapy, 12-year-old Wilma was able to walk normally again. But walking wasn't enough for Wilma, who was determined to be an athlete. Before long, her talent earned her a spot in the 1956 Olympics, where she earned a bronze medal. In the 1960 Olympics, the height of her career, she won three gold medals."

What is the main idea of this paragraph? You might be tempted to answer, "Wilma Rudolph" or "Wilma Rudolph's life." Yes, Wilma Rudolph's life is the **subject** of the passage—who or what the passage is about—but the subject is not necessarily the main idea. The **main idea** is what the writer wants to say about this subject. What is the main thing the writer says about Wilma's life?

Which of the following statements is the main idea of the paragraph?

a) Wilma Rudolph was very sick as a child.
b) Wilma Rudolph was an Olympic champion.
c) Wilma Rudolph is someone to admire.

**Main idea:** The overall fact, feeling, or thought a writer wants to convey about his or her subject.

The best answer is **c)**: Wilma Rudolph is someone to admire. This is the idea the paragraph adds up to; it's what holds all of the information in the paragraph together. This example also shows two important characteristics of a main idea:

1.  It is **general** enough to encompass all of the ideas in the passage.

2.  It is an **assertion.** An assertion is a statement made by the writer.

The main idea of a passage must be general enough to encompass all of the ideas in the passage. It should be broad enough for all of the other sentences in that passage to fit underneath it, like people under an umbrella. Notice that the first two options, "Wilma Rudolph was very sick as a child" and "Wilma Rudolph was an Olympic champion", are too specific to be the main idea. They aren't broad enough to cover all of the ideas in the passage, because the passage talks about both her illnesses and her Olympic achievements. Only the third answer is general enough to be the main idea of the paragraph.

A main idea is also some kind of **assertion** about the subject. An assertion is a claim that something is true. Assertions can be facts or opinions, but in either case, an assertion should be supported by specific ideas, facts, and details. In other words, the main idea makes a general assertion that tells readers that something is true.

The supporting sentences, on the other hand, show readers that this assertion is true by providing specific facts and details. For example, in the Wilma Rudolph paragraph, the writer makes a general assertion: "Wilma Rudolph, the crippled child who became an Olympic running champion, is an inspiration for us all." The other sentences offer specific facts and details that prove why Wilma Rudolph is an inspirational person.

Writers often state their main ideas in one or two sentences so that readers can have a very clear understanding about the main point of the passage. A sentence that expresses the main idea of a paragraph is called a **topic sentence.**

Notice, for example, how the first sentence in the Wilma Rudolph paragraph states the main idea:

> "Wilma Rudolph, the crippled child who became an Olympic running champion, is an inspiration for us all."

This sentence is therefore the topic sentence for the paragraph. Topic sentences are often found at the beginning of paragraphs. Sometimes, though, writers begin with specific supporting ideas and lead up to the main idea, and in this case the topic sentence is often found at the end of the paragraph. Sometimes the topic sentence is even found somewhere in the middle, and other times there isn't a clear topic sentence at all—but that doesn't mean there isn't a main idea; the author has just chosen not to express it in a clear topic sentence. In this last case, you'll have to look carefully at the paragraph for clues about the main idea.

## Main Ideas vs. Supporting Ideas

If you're not sure whether something is a main idea or a supporting idea, ask yourself the following question: is the sentence making a **general statement,** or is it providing **specific information?** In the Wilma Rudolph paragraph above, for example, all of the sentences except the first make specific statements. They are not general enough to serve as an umbrella or net for the whole paragraph.

Writers often provide clues that can help you distinguish between main ideas and their supporting ideas. Here are some of the most common words and phrases used to introduce specific examples:

1. **For example…**

2. **Specifically…**

3. **In addition…**

4. **Furthermore…**

5. **For instance…**

6. **Others…**

7. **In particular…**

8. **Some…**

These signal words tell you that a supporting fact or idea will follow. If you're having trouble finding the main idea of a paragraph, try eliminating sentences that begin with these phrases, because they will most likely be too specific to be a main ideas.

## Implied Main Idea

When the main idea is **implied**, there's no topic sentence, which means that finding the main idea requires some detective work. But don't worry! You already know the importance of structure, word choice, style, and tone. Plus, you know how to read carefully to find clues, and you know that these clues will help you figure out the main idea.

**For Example**:

"One of my summer reading books was *The Windows of Time.* Though it's more than 100 pages long, I read it in one afternoon. I couldn't wait to see what happened to Evelyn, the main character. But by the time I got to the end, I wondered if I should have spent my afternoon doing something else. The ending was so awful that I completely forgot that I'd enjoyed most of the book."

There's no topic sentence here, but you should still be able to find the main idea. Look carefully at what the writer says and how she says it. What is she suggesting?

  a) *The Windows of Time* is a terrific novel.
  b) *The Windows of Time* is disappointing.
  c) *The Windows of Time* is full of suspense.
  d) *The Windows of Time* is a lousy novel.

The correct answer is **b)** – the novel is disappointing. How can you tell that this is the main idea? First, we can eliminate choice **c)**, because it's too specific to be a main idea. It deals only with one specific aspect of the novel (its suspense).

Sentences **a)**, **b)**, and **d)**, on the other hand, all express a larger idea – a general assertion about the quality of the novel. But only one of these statements can actually serve as a "net" for the whole paragraph. Notice that while the first few sentences praise the novel, the last two criticize it. Clearly, this is a mixed review.

Therefore, the best answer is **b)**. Sentence **a)** is too positive and doesn't account for the "awful" ending. Sentence **d)**, on the other hand, is too negative and doesn't account for the reader's sense of suspense and interest in the main character. But sentence **b)** allows for both positive and negative aspects – when a good thing turns bad, we often feel disappointed.

Now let's look at another example. Here, the word choice will be more important, so read carefully.

> "Fortunately, none of Toby's friends had ever seen the apartment where Toby lived with his mother and sister. Sandwiched between two burnt-out buildings, his two-story apartment building was by far the ugliest one on the block. It was a real eyesore: peeling orange paint (orange!), broken windows, crooked steps, crooked everything. He could just imagine what his friends would say if they ever saw this poor excuse for a building."

Which of the following expresses the main idea of this paragraph?
  a) Toby wishes he could move to a nicer building.
  b) Toby wishes his dad still lived with them.
  c) Toby is glad none of his friends know where he lives.
  d) Toby is sad because he doesn't have any friends.

From the description, we can safely assume that Toby doesn't like his apartment building and wishes he could move to a nicer building **a)**. But that idea isn't general enough to cover the whole paragraph, because it's about his building.

Because the first sentence states that Toby has friends, the answer cannot be **d)**. We know that Toby lives only with his mother and little sister, so we might assume that he wishes his dad still lived with them, **b)**, but there's nothing in the paragraph to support that assumption, and this idea doesn't include the two main topics of the paragraph—Toby's building and Toby's friends.

What the paragraph adds up to is that Toby is terribly embarrassed about his building, and he's glad that none of his friends have seen it **c)**. This is the main idea. The paragraph opens with the word "fortunately," so we know that he thinks it's a good thing none of his friends have been to his house. Plus, notice how the building is described: "by far the ugliest on the block," which says a lot since it's stuck "between two burnt-out buildings." The writer calls it an "eyesore," and repeats "orange" with an exclamation point to emphasize how ugly the color is. Everything is "crooked" in this "poor excuse for a building." Toby is clearly ashamed of where he lives and worries about what his friends would think if they saw it.

## Cause and Effect

Understanding cause and effect is important for reading success. Every event has at least one cause (what made it happen) and at least one effect (the result of what happened). Some events have more than one cause, and some have more than one effect. An event is also often part of a chain of causes and effects. Causes and effects are usually signaled by important transitional words and phrases.

Words Indicating Cause:

1. **Because (of)**

2. **Created (by)**

3. **Caused (by)**

4. **Since**

Words Indicating Effect:

1. **As a result**

2. **Since**

3. **Consequently**

4. **So**

5. **Hence**

6. **Therefore**

Sometimes, a writer will offer his or her opinion about why an event happened when the facts of the cause(s) aren't clear. Or a writer may predict what he or she thinks will happen because of a certain event (its effects). If this is the case, you need to consider how reasonable those opinions are. Are the writer's ideas logical? Does the writer offer support for the conclusions he or she offers?

## Reading Between the Lines

Paying attention to word choice is particularly important when the main idea of a passage isn't clear. A writer's word choice doesn't just affect meaning; it also creates it. For example, look at the following description from a teacher's evaluation of a student applying to a special foreign language summer camp. There's no topic sentence, but if you use your powers of observation, you should be able to tell how the writer feels about her subject.

> "As a student, Jane usually completes her work on time and checks it carefully. She speaks French well and is learning to speak with less of an American accent. She has often been a big help to other students who are just beginning to learn the language."

What message does this passage send about Jane? Is she the best French student the writer has ever had? Is she one of the worst, or is she just average? To answer these questions, you have to make an inference, and you must support your inference with specific observations. What makes you come to the conclusion that you come to?

The **diction** of the paragraph above reveals that this is a positive evaluation, but not a glowing recommendation. Here are some of the specific observations you might have made to support this conclusion:

- The writer uses the word "usually" in the first sentence. This means that Jane is good about meeting deadlines for work, but not great; she doesn't always hand in her work on time.

- The first sentence also says that Jane checks her work carefully. While Jane may sometimes hand in work late, at least she always makes sure it's quality work. She's not sloppy.

- The second sentence tells us she's "learning to speak with less of an American accent." This suggests that she has a strong accent and needs to improve in this area. It also suggests, though, that she is already making progress.

- The third sentence tells us that she "often" helps "students who are just beginning to learn the language." From this we can conclude that Jane has indeed mastered the basics. Otherwise, how could she be a big help to students who are just starting to learn? By looking at the passage carefully, then, you can see how the writer feels about her subject.

# VOCABULARY

You may also be asked to provide definitions or intended meanings for words within passages. Some of those words, you may never have encountered before the test. But there are ways to answer correctly, and confidently, regardless!

## Context Clues

The most fundamental vocabulary skill is using the context of a word to determine its meaning. Your ability to observe sentences closely is extremely useful when it comes to understanding new vocabulary words.

### Types of Context
There are two different types of context that can help you understand the meaning of unfamiliar words: **sentence context** and **situational context**. Regardless of which context is present, these types of questions are not really testing your knowledge of vocabulary; rather, they test your ability to comprehend the meaning of a word through its usage.

> **Situational context** is context that comes from understanding the situation in which a word or phrase occurs.

> **Sentence context** occurs within the sentence that contains the vocabulary word. To figure out words using sentence context clues, you should first determine the most important words in the sentence.

> **Example:** I had a hard time reading her <u>illegible</u> handwriting.
> a) Neat.
> b) Unsafe.
> c) Sloppy.
> d) Educated.

> Already, you know that this sentence is discussing something that is hard to read. Look at the word that **illegible** is describing: **handwriting**. Based on context clues, you can tell that illegible means that her handwriting is hard to read.

> Next, look at the answer choices. Choice **a) Neat** is obviously a wrong answer because neat handwriting would not be difficult to read. Choice **b) Unsafe** and **d) Educated** don't make sense. Therefore, choice **c) Sloppy** is the best answer choice.

**Types of Clues**
There are four types of clues that can help you understand context, and therefore the meaning of a word. They are **restatement, positive/negative, contrast,** and **specific detail**.

**Restatement** clues occur when the definition of the word is clearly stated in the sentence.

> **Example**: The dog was <u>dauntless</u> in the face of danger, braving the fire to save the girl.
>   a) Difficult.
>   b) Fearless.
>   c) Imaginative.

Demonstrating **bravery** in the face of danger would be **fearless,** choice **b)**. In this case, the context clues tell you exactly what the word means.

**Positive/negative** clues can tell you whether a word has a positive or negative meaning.

> **Example**: The magazine gave a great review of the fashion show, stating the clothing was **sublime**.
>   a) Horrible.
>   b) Exotic.
>   c) Bland.
>   d) Gorgeous.

The sentence tells us that the author liked the clothing enough to write a **great** review, so you know that the best answer choice is going to be a positive word. Therefore, you can immediately rule out choices **a)** and **c)** because they are negative words. **Exotic** is a neutral word; alone, it doesn't inspire a **great** review. The most positive word is gorgeous, which makes choice **d) Gorgeous** the best answer.

The following sentence uses both restatement and positive/negative clues:

> "Janet suddenly found herself <u>destitute</u>, so poor she could barely afford to eat."

The second part of the sentence clearly indicates that destitute is a negative word; it also restates the meaning: very poor.

**Contrast clues** include the opposite meaning of a word. Words like **but, on the other hand,** and **however** are tip-offs that a sentence contains a contrast clue.

> **Example**: Beth did not spend any time preparing for the test, but Tyron kept a <u>rigorous</u> study schedule.
>   a) Strict.
>   b) Loose.
>   c) Boring.
>   d) Strange.

In this case, the word **but** tells us that Tyron studied in a different way than Beth. If Beth did not study very hard, then Tyron did study hard for the test. The best answer here, therefore, is choice **a) Strict**.

**Specific detail** clues give a precise detail that can help you understand the meaning of the word.

> **Example**: The box was heavier than he expected and it began to become <u>cumbersome</u>.
> a) Impossible.
> b) Burdensome.
> c) Obligated.
> d) Easier.

Start by looking at the specific details of the sentence. Choice **d)** can be eliminated right away because it is doubtful it would become **easier** to carry something that is **heavier**. There are also no clues in the sentence to indicate he was **obligated** to carry the box, so choice **c)** can also be disregarded. The sentence specifics, however, do tell you that the package was cumbersome because it was heavy to carry; this is a burden, which is **burdensome**, choice **b)**.

It is important to remember that more than one of these clues can be present in the same sentence. The more there are, the easier it will be to determine the meaning of the word, so look for them.

## Denotation and Connotation

As you know, many English words have more than one meaning. For example, the word **quack** has two distinct definitions: the sound a duck makes; and a person who publicly pretends to have a skill, knowledge, education, or qualification which they do not possess.

The **denotations** of a word are the dictionary definitions.

The **connotations** of a word are the implied meaning(s) or emotion which the word makes you think.

> **Example**: "Sure," Pam said excitedly, "I'd just love to join your club; it sounds so exciting!"

Now, read this sentence:

"Sure," Pam said sarcastically, "I'd just love to join your club; it sounds so exciting!"

Even though the two sentences only differ by one word, they have completely different meanings. The difference, of course, lies in the words "excitedly" and "sarcastically."

## Prefixes, Roots, and Suffixes

Although you are not expected to know every word in the English language for your test, you will need to have the ability to use deductive reasoning to find the choice that is the best match for the word in question, which is why we are going to explain how to break a word into its parts of meaning.

**prefix – root – suffix**

One trick in dividing a word into its parts is to first divide the word into its **syllables**. To show how syllables can help you find roots and affixes, we'll use the word **descendant,** which means one who comes from an ancestor. Start by dividing the word into its individual syllables; this word has three:

**de-scend-ant**.

The next step is to look at the beginning and end of the word, and then determine if these syllables are prefixes, suffixes, or possible roots. You can then use the meanings of each part to guide you in defining the word. When you divide words into their specific parts, they do not always add up to an exact definition, but you will see a relationship between their parts.

*Note*: This trick won't always work in every situation, because not all prefixes, roots, and suffixes have only one syllable. For example, take the word **monosyllabic** (which ironically means "one syllable"). There are five syllables in that word, but only three parts. The prefix is "mono," meaning "one." The root "syllab" refers to "syllable," while the suffix "ic" means "pertaining to." Therefore, we have – very ironically – one extremely long word which means "pertaining to one syllable."

**Roots**

Roots are the building blocks of all words. Every word is either a root itself or has a root. Just as a plant cannot grow without roots, neither can vocabulary, because a word must have a root to give it meaning.

**Example**: The test instructions were **unclear.**

The root is what is left when you strip away all the prefixes and suffixes from a word. In this case, take away the prefix "un-," and you have the root **clear.**

Roots are not always recognizable words, because they generally come from Latin or Greek words, such as **nat**, a Latin root meaning **born**. The word native, which means a person born of a referenced placed, comes from this root, so does the word prenatal, meaning before birth. Yet, if you used the prefix **nat** instead of born, just on its own, no one would know what you were talking about.

Words can also have more than one root. For example, the word **omnipotent** means all powerful. Omnipotent is a combination of the roots **omni-**, meaning all or every, and **-potent**, meaning power or strength. In this case, **omni** cannot be used on its own as a single word, but **potent** can.

Again, it is important to keep in mind that roots do not always match the exact definitions of words and they can have several different spellings, but breaking a word into its parts is still one of the best ways to determine its meaning.

**Prefixes**

Prefixes are syllables added to the beginning of a word and suffixes are syllables added to the end of the word. Both carry assigned meanings. The common name for prefixes and suffixes is **affixes**. Affixes do not have to be attached directly to a root and a word can often have more than one prefix and/or suffix.

Prefixes and suffixes can be attached to a word to completely change the word's meaning or to enhance the word's original meaning. Although they don't mean much to us on their own, when attached to other words affixes can make a world of difference.

Let's use the word **prefix** itself as an example:

**Fix** means to place something securely; and **Pre** means before. Therefore, **Prefix** means to place something before or in front.

**Suffixes**

Suffixes come after the root of a word.

**Example:** Feminism.

**Femin** is a root. It means female, woman.     **-ism** means act, practice or process. **Feminism** is the defining and establishing of equal political, economic, and social rights for women.

Unlike prefixes, **suffixes** can be used to change a word's part of speech.

**Example**: "Randy raced to the finish line." VS "Shana's costume was very racy."

In the first sentence, raced is a verb. In the second sentence, racy is an adjective. By changing the suffix from **-ed** to **-y**, the word race changes from a verb into an adjective, which has an entirely different meaning.

Although you cannot determine the meaning of a word by a prefix or suffix alone, you *can* use your knowledge of what root words mean to eliminate answer choices; indicating if the word is positive or negative can give you a partial meaning of the word.

# Test Your Knowledge: Language Arts – The Reading Section

*Questions 1 – 4 are based on the following passage:*

**From *"On Lying Awake at Night"* by Stewart Edward White (public domain):**

About once in so often you are due to lie awake at night. Why this is so I have never been able to discover. It apparently comes from no predisposing uneasiness of indigestion, no rashness in the matter of too much tea or tobacco, no excitation of unusual incident or stimulating conversation. In fact, you turn in with the expectation of rather a good night's rest. Almost at once the little noises of the forest grow larger, blend in the hollow bigness of the first drowse; your thoughts drift idly back and forth between reality and dream; when—*snap!*—you are broad awake!

For, unlike mere insomnia, lying awake at night in the woods is pleasant. The eager, nervous straining for sleep gives way to a delicious indifference. You do not care. Your mind is cradled in an exquisite poppy-suspension of judgment and of thought. Impressions slip vaguely into your consciousness and as vaguely out again. Sometimes they stand stark and naked for your inspection; sometimes they lose themselves in the mist of half-sleep. Always they lay soft velvet fingers on the drowsy imagination, so that in their caressing you feel the vaster spaces from which they have come. Peaceful-brooding your *faculties* receive. Hearing, sight, smell—all are preternaturally keen to whatever of sound and sight and woods perfume is abroad through the night; and yet at the same time active appreciation dozes, so these things lie on it sweet and cloying like fallen rose-leaves.

Nothing is more fantastically unreal to tell about, nothing more concretely real to experience, than this undernote of the quick water. And when you do lie awake at night, it is always making its unobtrusive appeal. Gradually its hypnotic spell works. The distant chimes ring louder and nearer as you cross the borderland of sleep. And then outside the tent some little woods noise snaps the thread. An owl hoots, a whippoorwill cries, a twig cracks beneath the cautious prowl of some night creature—at once the yellow sunlit French meadows puff away—you are staring at the blurred image of the moon spraying through the texture of your tent.

(You have cast from you with the warm blanket the drowsiness of dreams. A coolness, physical and spiritual, bathes you from head to foot. All your senses are keyed to the last vibrations. You hear the littler night prowlers; you glimpse the greater. A faint, searching woods perfume of dampness greets your nostrils. And somehow, mysteriously, in a manner not to be understood, the forces of the world seem in suspense, as though a touch might crystallize infinite possibilities into infinite power and motion. But the touch lacks. The forces hover on the edge of action, unheeding the little noises. In all humbleness and awe, you are a dweller of the Silent Places.

The night wind from the river, or from the open spaces of the wilds, chills you after a time. You begin to think of your blankets. In a few moments you roll yourself in their soft wool. Instantly it is morning.

And, strange to say, you have not to pay by going through the day unrefreshed. You may feel like turning in at eight instead of nine, and you may fall asleep with unusual promptitude, but your journey will begin clear-headedly, proceed springily, and end with much in reserve. No languor, no dull headache, no exhaustion, follows your experience. For this once your two hours of sleep have been as effective as nine.

1. In Paragraph 2, "faculties" is used to mean:
   a) Teachers.
   b) Senses.
   c) Imaginations.
   d) Capacities.

2. The author's opinion of insomnia is that:
   a) It is not a problem because nights without sleep are refreshing.
   b) It can happen more often when sleeping in the woods because of the noises in nature.
   c) It is generally unpleasant, but sometimes can be hypnotic.
   d) It is the best way to cultivate imagination.

3. By "strange to say" in Paragraph 6, the author means:
   a) The experience of the night before had an unreal quality.
   b) The language used in describing the night before is not easily understood.
   c) It is not considered acceptable to express the opinion the author expresses.
   d) Contrary to expectations, one is well-rested after the night before.

4. How is this essay best characterized?
   a) A playful examination of a common medical problem.
   b) A curious look at both sides of an issue.
   c) A fanciful description of the author's experience.
   d) A horrific depiction of night hallucinations.

*Questions 5-10 are based on the following passages:*

**Passage One**
**An excerpt from the essay "*Tradition and the Individual Talent*" by T.S. Eliot (public domain):**

No poet, no artist of any art, has his complete meaning alone. His significance, his appreciation is the appreciation of his relation to the dead poets and artists. You cannot value him alone; you must set him, for contrast and comparison, among the dead. I mean this as a principle of aesthetic, not merely historical, criticism. The necessity that he shall conform, that he shall cohere, is not one-sided; what happens when a new work of art is created is something that happens simultaneously to all the works of art which preceded it. The existing monuments form an ideal order among themselves, which is modified by the introduction of the new (the really new) work of art among them. The existing order is complete before the new work arrives; for order to persist after the supervention of novelty, the *whole* existing order must be, if ever so slightly, altered; and so the relations, proportions, values of each work of art toward the whole are readjusted; and this is conformity between the old and the new. Whoever has approved this idea of order, of the form of European, of English literature, will not find it preposterous that the past should be altered by the present as much as the present is directed by the past. And the poet who is aware of this will be aware of great difficulties and responsibilities.

**Passage Two**
**An excerpt from the Clive Bell's seminal art history book "*Art*" (public domain):**

To criticize a work of art historically is to play the science-besotted fool. No more disastrous theory ever issued from the brain of a charlatan than that of evolution in art. Giotto[1] did not creep, a grub, that Titian[2] might flaunt, a butterfly. To think of a man's art as leading on to the art of someone else is to misunderstand it. To praise or abuse or be interested in a work of art because it leads or does not lead to another work of art is to treat it as though it were not a work of art. The connection of one work of art with another may have everything to do with history: it has nothing to do with appreciation. So soon as we begin to consider a work as anything else than an end in itself we leave the world of art. Though the development of painting from Giotto to Titian may be interesting historically, it cannot affect the value of any particular picture: aesthetically, it is of no consequence whatever. Every work of art must be judged on its own merits.

**5.** In Passage One, the word "cohere" is used to most closely mean:
   a) To be congruous with.
   b) To supplant.
   c) To imitate.
   d) To overhaul.
   e) To deviate from.

**6.** In Passage Two, the author alludes to a butterfly to contradict which concept?
   a) The theory of evolution is responsible for the discipline of art criticism.
   b) Scientific knowledge is not necessary to understand paintings.
   c) Artists who show off are doomed to be criticized.
   d) Art which finds inspiration in nature is the highest form of art.
   e) Titian's art is beautiful as a result of the horrible art that came before.

**7.** The author of Passage One would be most likely to support:
   a) An artist who imitated the great works of the past.
   b) An art critic who relied solely on evaluating the aesthetics of new art.
   c) A historian who studied the aesthetic evolution of art.
   d) An artist who was also a scientist.
   e) An artist who shouldered the burden of creating something new, while affecting the old, in the world of art.

**8.** The meaning of the sentence "To praise or abuse or be interested in a work of art because it leads or does not lead to another work of art is to treat it as though it were not a work of art" in Passage 2 means:
   a) Works of art cannot be judged primarily by their relation to one another.
   b) One should not vandalize works of art.
   c) It is necessary to understand how one work of art leads to another in order to judge it.
   d) Works of art must be treated with respect.
   e) Understanding works of art is reliant on seeing them on a historical scale.

---

[1] Giotto was an Italian painter during the Middle Ages.
[2] Titian was an Italian painter during the Renaissance.

**9.** The author of Passage One would likely agree with which of the following statements?
- a) The past is a monument that is unalterable by the present.
- b) Historical knowledge is entirely separate from artistic knowledge.
- c) To understand a novel written in the twentieth century, it is necessary to have some knowledge of nineteenth century literature.
- d) Painters of Italian descent are all related to one another.
- e) One cannot be a scholar of literary history without also being a scholar of scientific thought.

**10.** The authors of both passages would likely agree with which of the following statements?
- a) An aesthetic judgment is the greatest possible approach to art criticism.
- b) Knowledge of history compromises one's ability to criticize works of art.
- c) The painter Titian was able to create his art as a consequence of the art which came before his time.
- d) It is imperative to understand the progression from one work of art to another.
- e) Not all works of art are consequential.

*Questions 11 and 12 are based on the following passage:*

**Excerpt from Anne Walker's "*A Matter of Proportion*," a short science-fiction story published in 1959 (public domain). In this excerpt, one character tells another about an injured man who is planning a secret operation:**

On the way, he filled in background. Scott had been living out of the hospital in a small apartment, enjoying as much liberty as he could manage. He had equipment so he could stump around, and an antique car specially equipped. He wasn't complimentary about them. Orthopedic products had to be: unreliable, hard to service, unsightly, intricate, and uncomfortable. If they also squeaked and cut your clothes, fine!

Having to plan every move with an eye on weather and a dozen other factors, he developed an uncanny foresight. Yet he had to improvise at a moment's notice. With life a continuous high-wire act, he trained every surviving fiber to precision, dexterity, and tenacity. Finally, he avoided help. Not pride, self-preservation; the compulsively helpful have rarely the wit to ask before rushing in to knock you on your face, so he learned to bide his time till the horizon was clear of beaming simpletons. Also, he found an interest in how far he could go.

**11.** Why does Scott primarily avoid the help of others?
- a) He has found that he is usually better off without it.
- b) He does not want to rely on other people for anything.
- c) He is doing experiments to test his own limits.
- d) He is working on a secret operation and cannot risk discovery.
- e) He does not realize that he needs assistance.

**12.** "Orthopedic" in paragraph one most nearly means:
   a) Uncomfortable.
   b) Dangerous.
   c) Corrective.
   d) Enhanced.
   e) Complicated.

*Questions 13 – 18 are based on the following passage:*

**Excerpt from Rennie W. Doane's *"Insects and Disease,"* a popular science account published in 1910 (public domain):**

It has been estimated that there are about four thousand species or kinds of Protozoans, about twenty-five thousand species of Mollusks, about ten thousand species of birds, about three thousand five hundred species of mammals, and from two hundred thousand to one million species of insects, or from two to five times as many kinds of insects as all other animals combined.

Not only do the insects preponderate in number of species, but the number of individuals belonging to many of the species is absolutely beyond our comprehension. Try to count the number of little green aphis on a single infested rose-bush, or on a cabbage plant; guess at the number of mosquitoes issuing each day from a good breeding-pond; estimate the number of scale insects on a single square inch of a tree badly infested with San José scale; then try to think how many more bushes or trees or ponds may be breeding their millions just as these and you will only begin to comprehend the meaning of this statement.

As long as these myriads of insects keep, in what we are pleased to call their proper place, we care not for their numbers and think little of them except as some student points out some wonderful thing about their structure, life-history or adaptations. But since the dawn of history we find accounts to show that insects have not always kept to their proper sphere but have insisted at various times and in various ways in interfering with man's plans and wishes, and on account of their excessive numbers the results have often been most disastrous.

Insects cause an annual loss to the people of the United States of over $1,000,000,000. Grain fields are devastated; orchards and gardens are destroyed or seriously affected; forests are made waste places and in scores of other ways these little pests which do not keep in their proper places are exacting this tremendous tax from our people. These things have been known and recognized for centuries, and scores of volumes have been written about the insects and their ways and of methods of combating them.

Yellow fever, while not so widespread as malaria, is more fatal and therefore more terrorizing. Its presence and spread are due entirely to a single species of mosquito, *Stegomyia calopus*. While this species is usually restricted to tropical or semi-tropical regions it sometimes makes its appearance in places farther north, especially in summer time, where it may thrive for a time. The adult mosquito is black, conspicuously marked with white. The legs and abdomen are banded with white and on the thorax is a series of white lines which in well-preserved specimens distinctly resembles a lyre. These mosquitoes are essentially domestic insects, for they are very rarely found except in houses or in their immediate vicinity. Once they enter a room they will scarcely leave it except to lay their eggs in a near-by cistern, water-pot, or some other convenient place.

Their habit of biting in the daytime has gained for them the name of "day mosquitoes" to distinguish them from the night feeders. But they will bite at night as well as by day and many other species are not at all adverse to a daylight meal, if the opportunity offers, so this habit is not distinctive. The recognition of these facts has a distinct bearing in the methods adopted to prevent the spread of yellow fever. There are no striking characters or habits in the larval or pupal stages that would enable us to distinguish without careful examination this species from other similar forms with which it might be associated. For some time it was claimed that this species would breed only in clean water, but it has been found that it is not nearly so particular, some even claiming that it prefers foul water. I have seen them breeding in countless thousands in company with *Stegomyia scutellaris* and *Culex fatigans* in the sewer drains in Tahiti in the streets of Papeete. As the larva feed largely on bacteria one would expect to find them in exactly such places where the bacteria are of course abundant. The fact that they are able to live in any kind of water and in a very small amount of it well adapts them to their habits of living about dwellings.

13. Why does the author list the amounts of different species of organisms in paragraph 1?
    a) To illustrate the vast number of species in the world.
    b) To demonstrate authority on the subject of insects.
    c) To establish the relative importance of mollusks and birds.
    d) To demonstrate the proportion of insects to other organisms.

14. What does the author use "their proper place" at the beginning of paragraph 3?
    a) The author is alluding to people's tendency to view insects as largely irrelevant to their lives.
    b) The author feels that insects belong only outdoors.
    c) The author wants the reader to feel superior to insects.
    d) The author is warning that insects can evolve to affect the course of human events.

15. This passage can be characterized primarily as:
    a) Pedantic.
    b) Droll.
    c) Informative.
    d) Abstract.
    e) Cautionary.

16. The main idea of this passage is best summarized as:
    a) Disease-carrying mosquitoes have adapted to best live near human settlements.
    b) Insects can have a detrimental effect on the economy by destroying crops.
    c) Insects are numerous in both types of species and individuals within a species.
    d) Although people do not always consider insects consequential, they can have substantial effects on human populations.

17. The use of "domestic" in Paragraph 5 most nearly means:
    a) Originating in the United States.
    b) Under the care of and bred by humans.
    c) Fearful of the outdoors.
    d) Living near human homes.

**18.** Which of the following ideas would best belong in this passage?
   a) An historical example of the effect a yellow fever outbreak had on civilization.
   b) A biological explanation of how diseases are transmitted from insects to humans.
   c) A reference to the numbers of insects which live far away from human habitation.
   d) Strategies for the prevention of yellow fever and malaria.


*Questions 19 – 26 are based on a long original passage (author Elissa Yeates):*

The collapse of the arbitrage[3] firm Long-Term Capital Management (LTCM) in 1998 is explained by a host of different factors: its investments were based on a high level of leverage, for example, and it was significantly impacted by Russia's default on the ruble. However, sociologist Donald MacKenzie maintains that the main factor in LTCM's demise was that, like all arbitrage firms, it was subjected to the sociological phenomena of the arbitrage community; namely, imitation. Arbitrageurs, who are generally known to one another as members of a specific subset of the financial society, use decision-making strategies based not only on mathematical models or pure textbook reason, but also based upon their feelings and gut reactions toward the financial market and on the actions of their peers. This imitation strategy leads to the overlapping "super portfolio," which creates an inherent instability that leads to collapse, the most infamous example being LTCM.

The public opinion of the partners of the firm in 1998 was that it had acted cavalierly with borrowed capital. However, in actuality the firm's strategy was exceedingly conservative, with a diversified portfolio, overestimated risks, and carefully hedged investments. The firm even tested tactics for dealing with financial emergencies such as the collapse of the European Monetary Union. Before the 1998 crisis, those in LTCM were never accused of recklessness. Nor were they, as is sometimes explained, overly reliant on mathematical models. The statistical hubris explanation falters under MacKenzie's evidence that John Meriwether and the others who ran the firm made their investment decisions based more upon their intricate understandings of the arbitrage market rather than upon the pure results of mathematical analyses. The financial instability that was created was not the result of the decision-making of one firm; but rather, the collective patterns of decision-making of all of
the arbitrage firms at the time.

The infamy of LTCM worked against the company. LTCM was composed of some of the most eminent minds in finance and it made devastating profits for the first few years that it was running. This led to imitation by other arbitrageurs who viewed the investments of LTCM as nearly sure bets. This type of replication of investment portfolios is not surprising, considering that arbitrageurs are all looking for similar types of pricing discrepancies and anomalies to exploit. The structure of arbitrageurs as a unique subset of the financial community who are largely personally known to one another further contributes to this phenomenon. Because of these factors over time the various players in the field of arbitrage created overlapping investments which MacKenzie dubs a "super portfolio." While LTCM alone may have created a geographically and industrially diverse portfolio, across the discipline of arbitrage as a whole capital flocked to similar investments.

Because of this super portfolio trend, multiple arbitrageurs were affected by the price changes of different assets caused by the actions of single independent firms. MacKenzie cites the example of the

---

[3] "Arbitrage" is a financial strategy which takes advantage of the temporary price differences of a single asset in different markets.

takeover of the investment bank Salomon Brothers by the Travelers Corporation. Salomon Brothers' portfolio, now under the management of someone who disliked the risks of arbitrage trading, liquidated its positions, which drove down the prices of assets in the markets in which it operated. The liquidation of the holdings of such a prominent player in the arbitrage game negatively affected the positions of every other firm that had a stake in those markets, including, of course, LTCM. This also illustrates the other sociological side of MacKenzie's argument: that arbitrageurs are subject to irrational internal pressures to cut their losses before their investments play out, which one of his interview subjects terms "queasiness" when faced with a stretch of losses.

**19.** The second paragraph of this passage primarily aims to:
   a) Explain that recklessness with borrowed capital is never profitable.
   b) Explore the factors ultimately responsible for the demise of the arbitrage firm Long-Term Capital Management.
   c) Demonstrate how the practice of arbitrage works.
   d) Laud the use of statistical models in calculating financial risks.
   e) Present and dismiss several theories of the collapse of Long-Term Capital Management.

**20.** In paragraph 2, "devastating" is used to mean:
   a) Destructive.
   b) Attractive.
   c) Blasphemous.
   d) Considerable.
   e) Appalling.

**21.** The final paragraph in this passage:
   a) Refutes the argument presented in the second paragraph of the passage.
   b) Gives a logical example of the phenomenon described in the introductory first paragraph of the passage.
   c) Contains an ardent plea against the passage of arbitrage.
   d) Gives a step-by-step account of the demise of Long-Term Capital Management.
   e) Argues that an understanding of sociology is crucial to successful financial practice.

**22.** Which of the following is a best description of the author's approach to the topic?
   a) Impassioned exposition.
   b) Curious exploration.
   c) Gleeful detection.
   d) Disgusted condemnation.
   e) Serene indifference.

**23.** Which of the following most accurately summarizes the author's thesis?
   a) If Long-Term Capital Management had developed a superportfolio, it would not have collapsed.
   b) Financial markets are inherently instable because those who participate in them are subject to human faults.
   c) Arbitrage firms should always endeavor to have geographically and industrially diverse investments.
   d) Long-Term Capital Management collapsed because arbitrageurs across the industry were investing in the same things, which caused instability.
   e) Long-Term Capital Management was run by financiers who were reckless and overly dependent on mathematical models, which is why it collapsed.

**24.** "Hubris" in paragraph 2 most likely means:
   a) Mathematical model.
   b) Reliance.
   c) Arrogance.
   d) Denial.
   e) Mistake.

**25.** Which of the following facts would undermine the main argument of the passage?
   a) The European Monetary Union was close to collapse in 1998.
   b) Some arbitrage firms steered clear of the practice of superportfolios.
   c) The Travelers Corporation was run by financiers who favored the practice of arbitrage.
   d) Arbitrageurs rarely communicate with one another or get information from the same source.
   e) Mathematical models used in finance in the 1990s were highly reliable.

**26.** Which of the following supports the argument made in the third paragraph?
   a) A detailed outline of the statistical models used by Long-Term Capital Management to make decisions.
   b) An explanation of how other arbitrage firms were able to learn the tactics practiced by Long-Term Capital Management.
   c) Examples of the differences between different investment portfolios of arbitrage firms.
   d) An outline of sociological theories about decision-making processes.
   e) A map showing the geographical diversity of arbitrage investors.

*Questions 27 – 36 are based on a long passage excerpted from Robert Louis Stevenson's classic novel* **Treasure Island** *(public domain). In this passage, the narrator tells about an old sailor staying at his family's inn.*

He had taken me aside one day and promised me a silver fourpenny on the first of every month if I would only keep my "weather-eye open for a seafaring man with one leg" and let him know the moment he appeared. Often enough when the first of the month came round and I applied to him for my wage, he would only blow through his nose at me and stare me down, but before the week was out he was sure to think better of it, bring me my fourpenny piece, and repeat his orders to look out for "the seafaring man with one leg."

How that personage haunted my dreams, I need scarcely tell you. On stormy nights, when the wind shook the four corners of the house and the surf roared along the cove and up the cliffs, I would see him in a thousand forms, and with a thousand diabolical expressions. Now the leg would be cut off at the knee, now at the hip; now he was a monstrous kind of a creature who had never had but the one leg, and that in the middle of his body. To see him leap and run and pursue me over hedge and ditch was the worst of nightmares. And altogether I paid pretty dear for my monthly fourpenny piece, in the shape of these abominable fancies.

But though I was so terrified by the idea of the seafaring man with one leg, I was far less afraid of the captain himself than anybody else who knew him. There were nights when he took a deal more rum and water than his head would carry; and then he would sometimes sit and sing his wicked, old, wild sea-songs, minding nobody; but sometimes he would call for glasses round and force all the trembling company to listen to his stories or bear a chorus to his singing. Often I have heard the house shaking with "Yo-ho-ho, and a bottle of rum," all the neighbors joining in for dear life, with the fear of death upon them, and each singing louder than the other to avoid remark. For in these fits he was the most overriding companion ever known; he would slap his hand on the table for silence all round; he would fly up in a passion of anger at a question, or sometimes because none was put, and so he judged the company was not following his story. Nor would he allow anyone to leave the inn till he had drunk himself sleepy and reeled off to bed.

His stories were what frightened people worst of all. Dreadful stories they were—about hanging, and walking the plank, and storms at sea, and the Dry Tortugas, and wild deeds and places on the Spanish Main. By his own account he must have lived his life among some of the wickedest men that God ever allowed upon the sea, and the language in which he told these stories shocked our plain country people almost as much as the crimes that he described. My father was always saying the inn would be ruined, for people would soon cease coming there to be tyrannized over and put down, and sent shivering to their beds; but I really believe his presence did us good. People were frightened at the time, but on looking back they rather liked it; it was a fine excitement in a quiet country life, and there was even a party of the younger men who pretended to admire him, calling him a "true sea-dog" and a "real old salt" and such like names, and saying there was the sort of man that made England terrible at sea.

In one way, indeed, he bade fair to ruin us, for he kept on staying week after week, and at last month after month, so that all the money had been long exhausted, and still my father never plucked up the heart to insist on having more. If ever he mentioned it, the captain blew through his nose so loudly that you might say he roared, and stared my poor father out of the room. I have seen him wringing his hands after such a rebuff, and I am sure the annoyance and the terror he lived in must have greatly hastened his early and unhappy death.

27. The purpose of Paragraph 3 is to:
    a) Illustrate how others view the captain.
    b) Explain the narrator's relationship with the captain.
    c) Give more background information about the inn where the narrator lives.
    d) Recount old seafaring lore.
    e) Explain why the captain is staying at this inn.

**28.** Which paragraph serves to evoke the life lived by sailors at sea?
   a) 1.
   b) 2.
   c) 3.
   d) 4.
   e) 5.

**29.** "Diabolical" in Paragraph 2 most nearly means:
   a) Angry.
   b) Judgmental.
   c) Contorted.
   d) Fiendish.
   e) Stoic.

**30.** What kind of character does the author reveal the captain to be the third paragraph?
   a) Temperamental.
   b) Generous.
   c) Jocund.
   d) Mysterious.
   e) Reserved.

**31.** What does the author reveal about the narrator in Paragraph 5?
   a) The narrator is afraid of the captain.
   b) The narrator is eager to go to sea.
   c) The narrator was often angry and annoyed.
   d) The narrator grew up in poverty.
   e) The narrator lost his father at an early age.

**32.** "Tyrannized" in Paragraph 4 is used to mean:
   a) Cajoled.
   b) Bullied.
   c) Frightened.
   d) Robbed.
   e) Ejected.

**33.** Which of the following statements about this passage is false?
   a) It is unclear whether the "seafaring man with one leg" actually exists.
   b) The narrator harbors a serious grudge against the captain.
   c) The narrator is interested in the captain's stories.
   d) The story takes place near the ocean.
   e) Most people who populate the story are afraid of the captain.

**34.** According to the captain, all of the following are hazards which can be encountered at sea EXCEPT:
- a) Hangings.
- b) Wicked men.
- c) Walking the plank.
- d) Storms.
- e) Sea monsters.

**35.** It can be inferred from the passage that:
- a) Singing was frowned upon in the community.
- b) The narrator never knew his mother.
- c) The narrator admired the captain.
- d) The captain is afraid of the seafaring man with one leg.
- e) The narrator went on to become a pirate.

**36.** By "they rather liked it" at the end of Paragraph 4, the author most closely means:
- a) The patrons of the inn enjoyed singing.
- b) The captain and others appreciated the rum available for sale at the inn.
- c) The narrator and his friends liked the stories the captain told.
- d) The captain provided entertainment at the inn, which would otherwise be boring.
- e) The narrator's parents liked having the captain around.

*Questions 37 – 40 are based on a short passage excerpted from the introduction to **The Best American Humorous Short Stories**, edited by Alexander Jessup (public domain).*

No book is duller than a book of jokes, for what is refreshing in small doses becomes nauseating when perused in large assignments. Humor in literature is at its best not when served merely by itself but when presented along with other ingredients of literary force in order to give a wide representation of life. Therefore "professional literary humorists," as they may be called, have not been much considered in making up this collection. In the history of American humor there are three names which stand out more prominently than all others before Mark Twain, who, however, also belongs to a wider classification: "Josh Billings" (Henry Wheeler Shaw, 1815-1885), "Petroleum V. Nasby" (David Ross Locke, 1833-1888), and "Artemus Ward" (Charles Farrar Browne, 1834-1867). In the history of American humor these names rank high; in the field of American literature and the American short story they do not rank so high. I have found nothing of theirs that was first-class both as humor and as short story. Perhaps just below these three should be mentioned George Horatio Derby (1823-1861), author of *Phoenixiana* (1855) and the *Squibob Papers* (1859), who wrote under the name "John Phoenix." As has been justly said, "Derby, Shaw, Locke and Browne carried to an extreme numerous tricks already invented by earlier American humorists, particularly the tricks of gigantic exaggeration and calm-faced mendacity, but they are plainly in the main channel of American humor, which had its origin in the first comments of settlers upon the conditions of the frontier, long drew its principal inspiration from the differences between that frontier and the more settled and compact regions of the country, and reached its highest development in Mark Twain, in his youth a child of the American frontier, admirer and imitator of Derby and Browne, and eventually a man of the world and one of its greatest humorists."

**37.** The author of this passage would disagree with all of the following statements EXCEPT:
   a) To be a successful storyteller, one must also be a professional literary humorist.
   b) Mark Twain is the most prominent American humorist.
   c) Lying with a straight face is a literary humorist device which had just been invented at the time this was published.
   d) The best joke books are the longest ones.
   e) Professional literary humorism is the highest form of writing.

**38.** The purpose of this passage is to:
   a) Scorn humorous writing as lesser than storytelling.
   b) Explain how writers use humorous literary devices.
   c) Provide contextual information about the landscape of American humorous writing.
   d) Make a case for the appreciation of the humorists Henry Shaw and David Locke.
   e) Deny the historical roots of American literary humor.

**39.** The word "prominently" in line four most closely means:
   a) Extravagantly.
   b) Inconspicuously.
   c) Significantly.
   d) Comically.
   e) Conceitedly.

**40.** Which of the following best summarizes the author's theory of the origins of American humorous writing?
   a) It started as a way of breaking away from British literary humor.
   b) It grew hand-in-hand with American storytelling.
   c) It was founded by Mark Twain.
   d) It was inspired by the differences between settlements and the frontier.
   e) It began with exaggerations and mendacity.

# Test Your Knowledge: Language Arts – The Reading Section – Answers

| | |
|---|---|
| 1. b) | 21. b) |
| 2. c) | 22. b) |
| 3. e) | 23. d) |
| 4. c) | 24. c) |
| 5. a) | 25. d) |
| 6. e) | 26. b) |
| 7. e) | 27. a) |
| 8. a) | 28. d) |
| 9. c) | 29. d) |
| 10. e) | 30. a) |
| 11. a) | 31. e) |
| 12. c) | 32. b) |
| 13. d) | 33. b) |
| 14. e) | 34. e) |
| 15. c) | 35. c) |
| 16. d) | 36. d) |
| 17. e) | 37. b) |
| 18. a) | 38. c) |
| 19. e) | 39. c) |
| 20. d) | 40. d) |

# Chapter 2: Language

This section is divided into two parts: a series of multiple-choice questions which will test your knowledge of grammar, structure, and syntax. You will have 55 minutes to answer 55 questions.

## Nouns, Pronouns, Verbs, Adjectives, and Adverbs

### Nouns
Nouns are people, places, or things. They are typically the subject of a sentence. For example, "The hospital was very clean." The noun is "hospital;" it is the "place."

### Pronouns
Pronouns essentially "replace" nouns. This allows a sentence to not sound repetitive. Take the sentence: "Sam stayed home from school because Sam was not feeling well." The word "Sam" appears twice in the same sentence. Instead, you can use a pronoun and say, "Sam stayed at home because *he* did not feel well." Sounds much better, right?

**Most Common Pronouns:**

- I, me, mine, my.

- You, your, yours.

- He, him, his.

- She, her, hers.

- It, its.

- We, us, our, ours.

- They, them, their, theirs.

### Verbs
Remember the old commercial, "Verb: It's what you do"? That sums up verbs in a nutshell! Verbs are the "action" of a sentence; verbs "do" things.

They can, however, be quite tricky. Depending on the subject of a sentence, the tense of the word (past, present, future, etc.), and whether or not they are regular or irregular, verbs have many variations.

**Example**: "He runs to second base." The verb is "runs." This is a "regular verb."

**Example**: "I am 7 years old." The verb in this case is "am." This is an "irregular verb."

As mentioned, verbs must use the correct tense – and that tense must remain the same throughout the sentence. "I was baking cookies and eat some dough." That sounded strange, didn't it? That's because the two verbs "baking" and "eat" are presented in different tenses. "Was baking" occurred in the past; "eat," on the other hand, occurs in the present. Instead, it should be "**ate** some dough."

## Adjectives

Adjectives are words that describe a noun and give more information. Take the sentence: "The boy hit the ball." If you want to know more about the noun "boy," then you could use an adjective to describe it. "The **little** boy hit the ball." An adjective simply provides more information about a noun or subject in a sentence.

## Adverb

For some reason, many people have a difficult time with adverbs – but don't worry! They are really quite simple. Adverbs are similar to adjectives in that they provide more information about a part of a sentence; however, they do **not** describe nouns – that's an adjective's job. Instead, adverbs describe verbs, adjectives, and even other adverbs.

Take the sentence: "The doctor said she hired a new employee."

It would give more information to say: "The doctor said she **recently** hired a new employee." Now we know more about *how* the action was executed. Adverbs typically describe when or how something has happened, how it looks, how it feels, etc.

### Good vs. Well

A very common mistake that people make concerning adverbs is the misuse of the word "good."

"Good" is an adjective – things taste good, look good, and smell good. "Good" can even be a noun – "Superman does good" – when the word is speaking about "good" vs. "evil." HOWEVER, "good" is never an adverb.

People commonly say things like, "I did really good on that test," or, "I'm good." Ugh! This is NOT the correct way to speak! In those sentences, the word "good" is being used to describe an action: how a person **did**, or how a person **is**. Therefore, the adverb "well" should be used. "I did really **well** on that test." "I'm **well**."

The correct use of "well" and "good" can make or break a person's impression of your grammar – make sure to always speak correctly!

## Study Tips for Improving Vocabulary and Grammar

1. Visit the Online Writing Lab website, which is sponsored by Purdue University, at http://owl.english.purdue.edu. This site provides you with an excellent overview of syntax, writing style, and strategy. It also has helpful and lengthy review sections that include multiple-choice "Test Your Knowledge" quizzes, which provide immediate answers to the questions.

2. It's beneficial to read the entire passage first to determine its intended meaning BEFORE you attempt to answer any questions. Doing so provides you with key insight into a passage's

syntax (especially verb tense, subject-verb agreement, modifier placement, writing style, and punctuation).

3. When you answer a question, use the "Process-of-Elimination Method" to determine the best answer. Try each of the four answers and determine which one BEST fits with the meaning of the paragraph. Find the BEST answer. Chances are that the BEST answer is the CORRECT answer.

## Practice Sentence Improvement

To give you a better idea of what you can expect from this section of the test, here are a few sample sentence improvement questions.

### Paragraph A
Of the two types of eclipses, the most common is the lunar eclipse, which occurs when a full moon passes through Earth's shadow. (1) The disc-shaped moon slowly disappears completely or turns a coppery red color. (2) Solar and lunar eclipses both occur from time to time. (3)

### Paragraph B
During a solar eclipse, the moon passes between the Earth and Sun. (4) As the moon moves into alignment, it blocks the light from the Sun creating an eerie darkness. (5) When the moon is perfectly in position, the Sun's light is visible as a ring, or corona, around the dark disc of the moon. (6) A lunar eclipse can be viewed from anywhere on the nighttime half of Earth, a solar eclipse can only be viewed from a zone that is only about 200 miles wide and covers about one-half of a percent of Earth's total area. (7)

1. Sentence 1: "Of the two types of eclipses, the most common is the lunar eclipse, which occurs when a full moon passes through Earth's shadow." What correction should be made to this sentence?
   a) Change "most" to "more."
   b) Change "occurs" to "occur."
   c) Change "which" to "that."
   d) Change "Earth's" to "Earths'."
   e) No correction is necessary.

2. Sentence 2: "The disc-shaped moon slowly disappears completely or turns a coppery red color." If you rewrote sentence 2, beginning with "The disc-shaped moon slowly turns a coppery red color," the next word should be:
   a) And.
   b) But.
   c) When.
   d) Because.
   e) Or.

3. Which revision would improve the effectiveness of paragraph A?
   a) Remove sentence 1.
   b) Move sentence 2 to the beginning of the paragraph.
   c) Remove sentence 2.
   d) Move sentence 3 to the beginning of the paragraph.
   e) No revision is necessary.

4. Sentence 7: "A lunar eclipse can be viewed from anywhere on the nighttime half of <u>Earth, a solar eclipse</u> can only be viewed from a zone that is only about 200 miles wide and covers about one-half of a percent of Earth's total area." Which of the following is the best way to write the underlined portion of this sentence? If the original is the best way, choose option **a)**.
   a) "Earth, a solar eclipse"
   b) "Earth a solar eclipse"
   c) "Earth; a solar eclipse"
   d) "Earth, because a solar eclipse"
   e) "Earth, when a solar eclipse"

**Answers:**

1. **a)**
   Use the comparative "more" when comparing only two things. Here, you comparing two types of eclipses, so "more" is correct. The other changes introduce errors.

2. **e)**
   The clauses are joined by the conjunction "or" in the original sentence. Maintaining this conjunction maintains the original relationship between ideas.

3. **d)**
   As sentence 3 would serve as a good topic sentence, as well as an effective lead into sentence 1, the paragraph could be improved by moving sentence 3 to the beginning.

4. **c)**
   The two related sentences should be separated by a semicolon. The other answers introduce incorrect punctuation or an inaccurate relationship between the sentences.

# Test Your Knowledge: Language Practice Test

*Questions 1 – 5 are based on the following original passage. Sentences are numbered at the end for easy reference within the questions.*

Examining the impact my lifestyle has on the earth's resources is, I believe, a fascinating and valuable thing to do (1). According to the Earth Day Network ecological footprint calculator, it would take four planet earths to sustain the human population if everyone used as many resources as I do (2). My "ecological footprint," or the amount of productive area of the earth that is required to produce the resources I consume, is therefore larger than the footprints of most of the population (3). It is hard to balance the luxuries and opportunities I have available to me with doing what I know to be better from an ecological standpoint (4).

It is fairly easy for me to recycle, so I do it, but it would be much harder to forgo the opportunity to travel by plane or eat my favorite fruits that have been flown to the supermarket from a different country (5). Although I get ecological points for my recycling habits, my use of public transportation, and living in an apartment complex rather than a free-standing residence, <u>my footprint expands when it is taken into account my not-entirely-local diet</u>, my occasional use of a car, my three magazine subscriptions, and my history of flying more than ten hours a year (6). I feel that realizing just how unfair my share of the earth's resources have been should help me to change at least some of my bad habits (7).

1.  Which of the following is the best version of sentence 1?
    a)  It is fascinating and valuable to examine the impact that my lifestyle has on the earth's resources.
    b)  Examining the impact my lifestyle has on the earth's resources is a fascinating and valuable thing to do.
    c)  To examine the impact my lifestyle has on the earth's resources is fascinating and is also valuable.
    d)  The impact of my lifestyle on the earth's resources is fascinating and valuable to examine.
    e)  Examining the impact my lifestyle has on the earth's resources is, I believe, a fascinating and valuable thing to do.

2.  Sentence 4 would best fit if it were moved where in this composition?
    a)  At the beginning of paragraph 2.
    b)  After sentence 5.
    c)  After sentence 6.
    d)  At the end of paragraph 2.
    e)  Sentence 4 is best left where it is.

3.  Which two sentences would be improved by switching positions?
    a)  1 and 2.
    b)  3 and 4.
    c)  5 and 6.
    d)  6 and 7.
    e)  2 and 7.

4. How could sentences 2 and 3 best be combined?
   a) According to the Earth Day Network ecological footprint calculator, it would take four planet earths to sustain the human population if everyone used as many resources as I do because I have a very large "ecological footprint," which is the amount of productive area of the earth that is required to produce the resources I consume.
   b) According to the Earth Day Network ecological footprint calculator, which calculates the amount of productive area of the earth that is required to produce the resources one consumes, it would take four planet earths to sustain the human population if everyone had a footprint as large as mine.
   c) According to the Earth Day Network ecological footprint calculator, it would take four planet earths to sustain the human population if everyone used as many resources as I do; my "ecological footprint," or the amount of productive area of the earth that is required to produce the resources I consume, is therefore larger than the footprints of most of the population.
   d) According to the Earth Day Network ecological footprint calculator, which measures the amount of productive area of the earth that is required to produce the resources a person consumes, my footprint is larger than that of most; it would take four planet earths to sustain the human population if everyone consumed as much as I do.
   e) According to the Earth Day Network ecological footprint calculator, my "ecological footprint," or the amount of productive area of the earth that is required to produce the resources I consume, would require four planet earths if it were to be the footprint of the human population; it is therefore larger than the footprints of most of the population.

5. Which of the following should replace the underlined portion of sentence 6?
   a) "my footprint expands when taken into account my not-entirely-local diet"
   b) "my footprint expands when taken into account are my not-entirely-local diet"
   c) "my footprint expands when we take into account my not-entirely-local diet"
   d) "my footprint expands when one takes into account my not-entirely-local diet"
   e) "my footprint expands when it is taken into account my not-entirely-local diet"

6. Which revision would most improve sentence 7?
   a) Eliminate the phrase "I feel that."
   b) Change "should help me" to "will help me."
   c) Add the phrase "In conclusion," to the beginning.
   d) Change "have been" to "has been."
   e) Eliminate the phrase "at least some of."

*Questions 7 – 12 are based on the short passage below, which is excerpted from Thomas Huxley's preface to his Collected Essays: Volume V (public domain) and modified slightly. Sentences are numbered at the end for easy reference within the questions.*

I had set out on a journey, with no other purpose than that of exploring a certain province of natural knowledge, I strayed no hair's breadth from the course which it was my right and my duty to pursue; and yet I found that, whatever route I took, before long, I came to a tall and formidable-looking fence (1). Confident I might be in the existence of an ancient and indefeasible right of way, before me stood the thorny barrier with its comminatory notice-board—"No Thoroughfare. By order" (2). There seemed no way over; nor did the prospect of creeping round, as I saw some do, attracts me (3). True there was no longer any cause to fear the spring guns and man-traps set by former lords of the manor; but one is apt to get very dirty going on all-fours (4). The only alternatives were either to give up my journey—which I was not minded to do—or to break the fence down and go through it (5). I swiftly ruled out crawling under as an option (6). I also ruled out turning back (7).

7. How could sentence 1 best be changed?
   a) The comma after journey should be removed.
   b) The comma after knowledge should be changed to a semicolon.
   c) "and yet" should be eliminated.
   d) Change "I had set out" to "I set out."
   e) No change.

8. Sentence 6 should be placed where in the passage?
   a) After sentence 1.
   b) After sentence 2.
   c) After sentence 3.
   d) After sentence 4.
   e) Left after sentence 5.

9. Which edit should be made in sentence 3?
   a) "nor" should be changed to "or."
   b) "seemed" should be changed to "seems."
   c) "me" should be changed to "I."
   d) "attracts" should be changed to "attract."
   e) No edit should be made.

10. How could sentences 6 and 7 best be combined?
   a) Swiftly, I ruled out crawling under as an option and also turning back.
   b) Ruling out two options swiftly: crawling under and turning back.
   c) I swiftly ruled out the options of crawling under or turning back.
   d) I ruled out crawling under as an option and I swiftly also ruled out turning back.
   e) I swiftly ruled out crawling under as an option and also turning back.

**11.** Which word could be inserted at the beginning of sentence 2 before "confident" to best clarify the meaning?

    a) Even.

    b) However.

    c) Hardly.

    d) Finally.

    e) Especially.

**12.** Which of the following is the best way to split sentence 1 into two separate sentences?

    a) I had set out on a journey, with no other purpose than that of exploring a certain province of natural knowledge. I strayed no hair's breadth from the course which it was my right and my duty to pursue; and yet I found that, whatever route I took, before long, I came to a tall and formidable-looking fence.

    b) I had set out on a journey, with no other purpose than that of exploring a certain province of natural knowledge, I strayed no hair's breadth from the course which it was my right and my duty to pursue. Yet I found that, whatever route I took, before long, I came to a tall and formidable-looking fence.

    c) I had set out on a journey, with no other purpose than that of exploring a certain province of natural knowledge, I strayed no hair's breadth from the course which it was my right and my duty to pursue; and yet I found that, whatever route I took, before long. I came to a tall and formidable-looking fence.

    d) I had set out on a journey. With no other purpose than that of exploring a certain province of natural knowledge, I strayed no hair's breadth from the course which it was my right and my duty to pursue; and yet I found that, whatever route I took, before long, I came to a tall and formidable-looking fence.

    e) I had set out on a journey, with no other purpose than that of exploring a certain province of natural knowledge, I strayed no hair's breadth from the course which it was my right and my duty to pursue; and yet. I found that, whatever route I took, before long, I came to a tall and formidable-looking fence.

*Questions 13 – 27 are based on the short passage below:*

Sandra Cisneros, perhaps the best known Latina author in the United States, writes poems and stories whose titles alone – "Barbie-Q," "My Lucy Friend Who Smells Like Corn," "Woman Hollering Creek" – engage potential readers' curiosity. (1) Ironically, this renowned writer, whose books are printed on recycled paper, did not do wellin school. (2) When she lectures at schools and public libraries, Cisneros presents the evidence. (3) An elementary school report card containing Cs, Ds and a solitary B (for conduct). (4) Cisneros has a theory to explain her low grades: teachers had low expectations for Latina and Latino students from Chicago's South Side. (5) Despite the obstacles that she faced in school, Cisneros completed not only high school but also college. (6) Her persistence paid off in her twenties, when Cisneros was admitted <u>prestigious</u> to the Writers' Workshop at the University of Iowa. (7)

Cisneros <u>soon</u> observed that most of her classmates at the university seemed to have a common set of memories, based on middle-class childhoods, from which to draw in their writing. (8) Cisneros felt <u>decided</u> out of place. _____("9A")_____. (9) She decided to speak from her own experience. (10) Her voice, which by being one of a Latina living outside of the mainstream, found a large and attentive audience in 1984 with the publication of her first short story collection, The House on Mango Street. (11) <u>Today</u> the book is read by middle school, high school, and college students across the United States. (12) Cisneros uses her influence as a successful writer to help other Latina and Latino writers get their works published. (13) But <u>having made the argument that,</u> in order for large numbers of young Latinos to achieve literary success, the educational system itself must change. (14) Cisneros <u>hints</u> that she succeeded in spite of the educational system. "I'm the exception," she insists, "not the rule." (15)

**13.** What change should be made to sentence 1?
   a) No Change.
   b) "author and writer."
   c) "author and novelist."
   d) "wordsmith and author."

**14.** What change should be made towards the end of sentence 1?
   a) No Change.
   b) "potential, reader's."
   c) "potential, readers."
   d) "potential readers."

**15.** What change should be made to sentence 2?
   a) No Change.
   b) "writer, who is recognized by her orange and black eyeglasses"
   c) "writer, who likes to write at night,"
   d) "writer"

**16.** What change should be made to sentence 3?
   a) No Change.
   b) "evidence: an"
   c) "evidence; an"
   d) "evidence an"

**17.** The best placement for the underlined portion in sentence 7 would be:
   a) Where it is now.
   b) Before the word admitted.
   c) Before the word "Writers'."
   d) Before the word "Workshop."

**18.** Which word would best replace the underlined portion in sentence 8?
   a) No Change.
   b) "furthermore"
   c) "nevertheless"
   d) "therefore"

**19.** Which of the following is the best beginning of sentence 9?
   a) No Change.
   b) "Cisneros herself,"
   c) "Cisneros, herself"
   d) "Cisneros,"

**20.** Which of the following is should replace the underlined word in sentence 9?
   a) No Change.
   b) "deciding"
   c) "decidedly"
   d) "decidedly and"

**21.** Which of the following true statements, if added at _____("9A")_____ , would best serve as a transition between the challenges Cisneros faced as an aspiring writer and her success in meeting those challenges?
   a) "She did not know what to do."
   b) "Then she had a break through."
   c) "At that point she almost went home to Chicago."
   d) "She wondered whether she was in the right field."

**22.** Which of the following changes should be made to sentence 11?
   a) No Change.
   b) "voice – that of a Latina living outside the  mainstream –"
   c) "voice, being one of a Latina living outside the mainstream, it"
   d) "voice – in which it was a Latina living outside the mainstream –"

**23.** Which of the following changes should be made to sentence 11?
   a) No Change.
   b) "1984, With"
   c) "1984; with"
   d) "1984, with,"

**24.** Which of the following is the best change to the underlined word at the beginning of sentence 12?
   a) No Change.
   b) "In the future,"
   c) "Meanwhile,"
   d) "At the same time,"

**25.** Which of the following is the best replacement for the underlined portion in sentence 14?
   a) No Change.
   b) "she argues that,"
   c) "arguing that,"
   d) "she argues that, when"

**26.** Which choice best shows that Cisneros is emphatic about expressing the belief stated in the underlined portion of sentence 15?
   a) No Change.
   b) "Says."
   c) "Supposes."
   d) "Asserts."

**27.** The writer is considering deleting the last sentence. If the writer decided to delete this sentence, the paragraph would primarily lose a statement that:
   a) Enhances the subject and setting.
   b) Provides support for a point previously made.
   c) Humorously digresses from the main topic of the paragraph.
   d) Contradicts Cisneros's claim made earlier in the essay.


*Questions 28-40 are based on the short passage below:*

Traveling on commercial airlines has changed substantially <u>over years</u>. (1) When commercial air travel first became available, it was so expensive that usually only businessmen could afford <u>to do so</u>. (2) Airplane efficiency, the relative cost of fossil fuels, <u>and using economies</u> of scale have all contributed to make travel by air more affordable and common. (3) These days, there are nearly 30,000 commercial air flights in the world each day! (4)

Depending on the size of the airport you are departing from, you should arrive 90 minutes to two and a half hours before your plane leaves. (5) Things like checking your luggage and flying internationally can make the process of getting to your gate take longer. (6) If you fly out of a very busy airport, like <u>LaGuardia, in</u> New York City, on a very busy travel day, like the day before Thanksgiving, you can easily miss your flight if you don't arrive early enough. (7)

Security processes for passengers have also changed. (8) In the 1960s, there was <u>hardly any</u> security: you could just buy your ticket and walk on to the plane the day of the flight without even needing to show identification. (9) In the 1970s, American commercial airlines started installing sky marshals on many <u>flights, an</u> undercover law enforcement officers who would protect the passengers from a potential hijacking. (10)

Also in the early 1970s, the federal government began to require that airlines screen passengers and their luggage for things like weapons and bombs. (11) After the 2001 terrorist attacks in the United States, these requirements were <u>stringently enforced</u>. (12) Family members can no longer meet someone at the <u>gate; only ticketed passengers are allowed into the gate area</u>. (13) The definition of <u>weapons are</u> not allowed is expanded every time there is a new incident for example liquids are now restricted on planes after an attempted planned attack using gel explosives in 2006. (14)

Despite the hassles of traveling by air, it is still a boon to modern <u>life. (15)</u> <u>Still, some</u> businesses are moving away from sending employees on airplane trips, <u>as</u> face-to-face video conferencing technologies improve. (16) A trip which might take ten hours by car <u>can take only</u> two hours by plane. (17) However, the ability to travel quickly by air <u>will always be valued, by citizens</u> of our modern society. (18)

**28.** Which of the following is the best change to the underlined portion of sentence 1?
- a) No Change.
- b) "over the years"
- c) "over time"
- d) Delete.

**29.** Which of the following is the best change to the underlined portion of sentence 2?
- a) No Change.
- b) "to do it"
- c) "to fly"
- d) "do so"

**30.** Which of the following is the best change to the underlined portion of sentence 3?
- a) No Change.
- b) "using economies"
- c) "and the use of economies"
- d) "and economies"

**31.** Which of the following is the best change to the underlined portion of sentence 7?
- a) No Change.
- b) "La Guardia in"
- c) "La Guardia; in"
- d) "La Guardia,"

**32.** Which of the following is the best change to the underlined portion of sentence 9?
- a) No Change.
- b) "hardly"
- c) "no"
- d) "barely"

**33.** Which of the following is the best change to the underlined portion of sentence 10?
- a) No Change.
- b) "flights; an"
- c) "flights. Marshals are"
- d) "flights, marshals are"

**34.** Which of the following is the best change to the underlined portion of sentence 12?
- a) No Change.
- b) "stiffly upheld"
- c) "enforced with more stringency"
- d) "more stringently enforced"

**35.** If the underlined portion in sentence 13 were deleted, the passage would lose:
   a) No Change.
   b) An explanation of the screening process.
   c) Ambiguity over why family members are no longer allowed at the gate.
   d) A further specific example of how regulations have changed over time.

**36.** Which of the following is the best change to the underlined portion in sentence 14?
   a) No Change.
   b) "weapon is"
   c) "weapons"
   d) "weapons which are"

**37.** Which of the following is the proper transition between sentences 15 & 16?
   a) No Change.
   b) "life. Some"
   c) "life even though some"
   d) "life, still some"

**38.** Which of the following is the best replacement for the underlined word in sentence 16?
   a) No Change.
   b) "because"
   c) "while"
   d) "since"

**39.** Which of the following is the best change to the underlined portion in sentence 17?
   a) No Change.
   b) "may only take"
   c) "takes only"
   d) "will only take"

**40.** Which of the following is the best change to the underlined portion in sentence 18?
   a) No Change.
   b) "citizens will always value"
   c) "will always, be valued by citizens"
   d) "will always be valued by citizens"

# Test Your Knowledge: Language – Answers

| | |
|---|---|
| 1.  a). | 21. b). |
| 2.  c). | 22. b). |
| 3.  c). | 23. a). |
| 4.  d). | 24. a). |
| 5.  d). | 25. b). |
| 6.  d). | 26. d). |
| 7.  b). | 27. b). |
| 8.  d). | 28. b). |
| 9.  d). | 29. c). |
| 10. c). | 30. c). |
| 11. b). | 31. b). |
| 12. a). | 32. a). |
| 13. a). | 33. c). |
| 14. a). | 34. d). |
| 15. d). | 35. d). |
| 16. b). | 36. d). |
| 17. c). | 37. c). |
| 18. a). | 38. a). |
| 19. a). | 39. b). |
| 20. c). | 40. d). |

# Chapter 3: Mathematics

Do not over think the differences between the Math Comprehension and Math Application sections on the TABE test. They both require the same fundamental mathematical knowledge, covering various concepts such as: numbers and operations, algebra, geometry, data analysis, statistics, and probability.

Before you take the TABE test, you want to make sure that you have a good understanding of those math areas which will be covered. You will need to sharpen your skills – and we'll provide you with the knowledge that you'll need for the test.

## Math Concepts Tested

You have a much better chance of getting a good score if you know what to expect. The test covers math up to and including the first semester of Algebra II, as well as fundamental geometry. You will not be given any formulas, such as those required for geometric calculations, so make sure to study them until they are solidified concepts in your mind.

Here is a breakdown of areas covered:

### Numbers and Operations
- Absolute values, inequalities, probabilities, exponents, and radicals.

### Algebra and Functions
- Basic equation-solving, simultaneous equations, binomials & polynomials, and inequalities.

### Geometry and Measurement
- Angle relationships, area and perimeter of geometric shapes, and volume.

Math skills that you won't need:

- Working with bulky numbers or endless calculations.
- Working with imaginary numbers or the square roots of negative numbers.
- Trigonometry or calculus.

## The Most Common Mistakes

People make mistakes all the time – but during a test, those mistakes can cost you a passing score. Watch out for these common mistakes that people make:

- Answering with the wrong sign (positive / negative).

- Mixing up the Order of Operations.

- Misplacing a decimal.

- Not reading the question thoroughly (and therefore providing an answer that was not asked for.)

- Circling the wrong letter, or filling in wrong circle choice.

If you're thinking, "Those ideas are just common sense" – exactly! Most of the mistakes made are simple mistakes. Regardless, they still result in a wrong answer and the loss of a potential point.

## Helpful Strategies

1. **Go Back to the Basics**: First and foremost, practice your basic skills: sign changes, order of operations, simplifying fractions, and equation manipulation. These are the skills used most on the test, though they are applied in different contexts. Remember that when it comes right down to it, all math problems rely on the four basic skills of addition, subtraction, multiplication, and division. All that changes is the order in which they are used to solve a problem.

2. **Don't Rely on Mental Math**: Using mental math is great for eliminating answer choices, but ALWAYS WRITE IT DOWN! This cannot be stressed enough. Use whatever paper is provided; by writing and/or drawing out the problem, you are more likely to catch any mistakes. The act of writing things down forces you to organize your calculations, leading to an improvement in your score.

3. **The Three-Times Rule**:

   - **Step One – Read the question**: Write out the given information.

   - **Step Two – Read the question**: Set up your equation(s) and solve.

   - **Step Three – Read the question:** Make sure that your answer makes sense (is the amount too large or small; is the answer in the correct unit of measure; etc.).

4. **Make an Educated Guess**: Eliminate those answer choices which you are relatively sure are incorrect, and then guess from the remaining choices. Educated guessing is critical to increasing your score.

## Math Formulas, Facts, and Terms that You Need to Know

The next few pages will cover the various math subjects (starting with the basics, but in no particular order) along with worked examples. Use this guide to determine the areas in which you need more review and work these areas first. You should take your time at first and let your brain recall the math necessary to solve the problems, using the examples given to remember these skills.

## Order of Operations

**PEMDAS** – Parentheses/Exponents/**M**ultiply/**D**ivide/**A**dd/**S**ubtract

Perform the operations within parentheses first, and then any exponents. After those steps, perform all multiplication and division. (These are done from left to right, as they appear in the problem) Finally, do all required addition and subtraction, also from left to right as they appear in the problem.

**Example**: Solve $(-(2)^2 - (4 + 7))$.
$(-4 - 11) = -15$.

**Example**: Solve $((5)^2 \div 5 + 4 * 2)$.
$25 \div 5 + 4 * 2$.

$5 + 8 = 13$.

## Positive & Negative Number Rules

$(+) + (-)$ = Subtract the two numbers. Solution gets the sign of the larger number.

$(-) + (-)$ = Negative number.

$(-) * (-)$ = Positive number.

$(-) * (+)$ = Negative number.

$(-) / (-)$ = Positive number.

$(-) / (+)$ = Negative number.

## Greatest Common Factor (GCF)

The greatest factor that divides two numbers.

**Example**: The GCF of 24 and 18 is 6. 6 is the largest number, or greatest factor, that can divide both 24 and 18.

## Geometric Sequence

Each term is equal to the previous term multiplied by $x$.

**Example**: 2, 4, 8, 16.

$x = 2$.

## Fractions

Adding and subtracting fractions requires a common denominator.

Find a common denominator for:

$$\frac{2}{3} - \frac{1}{5}$$

$$\frac{2}{3} - \frac{1}{5} = \frac{2}{3}\left(\frac{5}{5}\right) - \frac{1}{5}\left(\frac{3}{3}\right) = \frac{10}{15} - \frac{3}{15} = \frac{7}{15}$$

To add mixed fractions, work first the whole numbers, and then the fractions.

$$2\frac{1}{4} + 1\frac{3}{4} = 3\frac{4}{4} = 4$$

To subtract mixed fractions, convert to single fractions by multiplying the whole number by the denominator and adding the numerator. Then work as above.

$$2\frac{1}{4} - 1\frac{3}{4} = \frac{9}{4} - \frac{7}{4} = \frac{2}{4} = \frac{1}{2}$$

To multiply fractions, convert any mixed fractions into single fractions and multiply across; reduce to lowest terms if needed.

$$2\frac{1}{4} * 1\frac{3}{4} = \frac{9}{4} * \frac{7}{4} = \frac{63}{16} = 3\frac{15}{16}$$

To divide fractions, convert any mixed fractions into single fractions, flip the second fraction, and then multiply across.

$$2\frac{1}{4} \div 1\frac{3}{4} = \frac{9}{4} \div \frac{7}{4} = \frac{9}{4} * \frac{4}{7} = \frac{36}{28} = 1\frac{8}{28} = 1\frac{2}{7}$$

## Probabilities

A probability is found by dividing the number of desired outcomes by the number of possible outcomes. (The piece divided by the whole.)

**Example**: What is the probability of picking a blue marble if 3 of the 15 marbles are blue?

3/15 = 1/5. The probability is **1 in 5** that a blue marble is picked.

## Prime Factorization

Expand to prime number factors.

**Example**: 104 = 2 * 2 * 2 * 13.

## Absolute Value

The absolute value of a number is its distance from zero, not its value.

So in $|x| = a$, "$x$" will equal "$-a$" as well as "$a$."

Likewise, $|\,3\,| = 3$, and $|{-3}| = 3$.

Equations with absolute values will have two answers. Solve each absolute value possibility separately. All solutions must be checked into the original equation.

> **Example:** Solve for $x$:
> $|2x - 3| = x + 1$.
>
> Equation One: $2x - 3 = -(x + 1)$.
> $\quad\quad\quad\quad\quad 2x - 3 = -x - 1$.
> $\quad\quad\quad\quad\quad 3x = 2$.
> $\quad\quad\quad\quad\quad \mathbf{x = 2/3}$.
>
> Equation Two: $2x - 3 = x + 1$.
> $\quad\quad\quad\quad\quad \mathbf{x = 4}$.

## Mean, Median, Mode

**Mean** is a math term for "average." Total all terms and divide by the number of terms.

Find the mean of 24, 27, and 18.

$24 + 27 + 18 = 69 \div 3 = \mathbf{23}$.

**Median** is the middle number of a given set, found after the numbers have all been put in numerical order. In the case of a set of even numbers, the middle two numbers are averaged.

What is the median of 24, 27, and 18?

18, **24**, 27.

What is the median of 24, 27, 18, and 19?

18, 19, 24, 27 ($19 + 24 = 43$. $43/2 = \mathbf{21.5}$).

**Mode** is the number which occurs most frequently within a given set.

What is the mode of 2, 5, 4, 4, 3, 2, 8, 9, 2, 7, 2, and 2?

The mode would be **2** because it appears the most within the set.

## Exponent Rules

| Rule | Example |
|---|---|
| $x^0 = 1$ | $5^0 = 1$ |
| $x^1 = x$ | $5^1 = 5$ |
| $x^a \cdot x^b = x^{a+b}$ | $5^2 * 5^3 = 5^5$ |
| $(xy)^a = x^a y^a$ | $(5 * 6)^2 = 5^2 * 6^2 = 25 * 36$ |
| $(x^a)^b = x^{ab}$ | $(5^2)^3 = 5^6$ |
| $(x/y)^a = x^a/y^a$ | $(10/5)^2 = 10^2/5^2 = 100/25$ |
| $x^a/y^b = x^{a-b}$ | $5^4/5^3 = 5^1 = 5$  (remember $x \neq 0$) |
| $x^{1/a} = \sqrt[a]{x}$ | $25^{1/2} = \sqrt[2]{25} = 5$ |
| $x^{-a} = \dfrac{1}{x^a}$ | $5^{-2} = \frac{1}{5^2} = \frac{1}{25}$ (remember $x \neq 0$) |
| $(-x)^a$ = positive number if "a" is even; negative number if "a" is odd. | |

## Roots

Root of a Product:  $\sqrt[n]{a \cdot b} = \sqrt[n]{a} \cdot \sqrt[n]{b}$

Root of a Quotient:  $\sqrt[n]{\dfrac{a}{b}} = \dfrac{\sqrt[n]{a}}{\sqrt[n]{b}}$

Fractional Exponent:  $\sqrt[n]{a^m} = a^{m/n}$

## Literal Equations

Equations with more than one variable. Solve in terms of one variable first.

**Example**: Solve for $y$: $4x + 3y = 3x + 2y$.

Step 1 – Combine like terms: $3y - 2y = 4x - 2x$.

Step 2 – Solve for $y$: $y = 2x$.

## Midpoint

To determine the midpoint between two points, simply add the two $x$ coordinates together and divide by 2 (midpoint $x$). Then add the $y$ coordinates together and divide by 2 (midpoint $y$).

$$\left( \frac{x_1 + x_2}{2}, \frac{y_1 + y}{2} \right)$$

## Slope

The formula used to calculate the slope ($m$) of a straight line connecting two points is: $m = (y_2 - y_1) / (x_2 - x_1)$ = change in $y$ / change in $x$.

**Example**: Calculate slope of the line in the diagram:

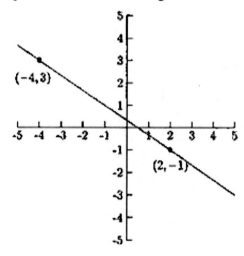

$m = (3 - (-1))/(-4 - 2) = 4/-6 = $ **- 2/3.**

## Inequalities

Inequalities are solved like linear and algebraic equations, except the sign must be reversed when dividing by a negative number.

**Example**: $-7x + 2 < 6 - 5x$.

Step 1 – Combine like terms: $-2x < 4$.

Step 2 – Solve for x. (Reverse the sign): **$x > $ -2.**

Solving compound inequalities will give you two answers.

**Example**: $-4 \leq 2x - 2 \leq 6$.

Step 1 – Add 2 to each term to isolate $x$: $-2 \leq 2x \leq 8$.

Step 2: Divide by 2: $-1 \leq x \leq 4$.

Solution set is **[-1, 4]**.

**Algebraic Equations**

When simplifying or solving algebraic equations, you need to be able to utilize all math rules: exponents, roots, negatives, order of operations, etc.

1. Add & Subtract: Only the coefficients of like terms.

   **Example**: $5xy + 7y + 2yz + 11xy - 5yz = 16xy + 7y - 3yz$.

2. Multiplication: First the coefficients then the variables.

   **Example**: Monomial * Monomial.

   $(3x^4y^2z)(2y^4z^5) = 6x^4y^6z^6$.

   (A variable with no exponent has an implied exponent of 1.)

   **Example**: Monomial * Polynomial.

   $(2y^2)(y^3 + 2xy^2z + 4z) = 2y^5 + 4xy^4z + 8y^2z$.

   **Example**: Binomial * Binomial.

   $(5x + 2)(3x + 3)$.

   (Remember FOIL – First, Outer, Inner, Last.)

   First: $5x * 3x = 15x^2$.

   Outer: $5x * 3 = 15x$.

   Inner: $2 * 3x = 6x$.

   Last: $2 * 3 = 6$.

   Combine like terms: $15x^2 + 21x + 6$.

   **Example**: Binomial * Polynomial.

   $(x + 3)(2x^2 - 5x - 2)$.

   First term: $x(2x^2 - 5x - 2) = 2x^3 - 5x^2 - 2x$.

   Second term: $3(2x^2 - 5x - 2) = 6x^2 - 15x - 6$.

   Added Together: $2x^3 + x^2 - 17x - 6$.

## Distributive Property

When a variable is placed outside of a parenthetical set, it is *distributed* to all of the variables within that set.

$5(2y - 3x) = 10y - 15x$ [Can also be written as $(2y - 3x)5$].

$2x(3y + 1) + 6x = 6xy + 2x + 6x = 6xy + 8x$.

## Combining Like Terms

This is exactly how it sounds! When a variable ($x$, $y$, $z$, $r$ – anything!) is present in an equation, you can combine those terms with like variables.

$9r + 2r = 11r$.

$4x + 2y + 3 - 2x = 2x + 2y + 3$.

## Arithmetic Sequence

Each term is equal to the previous term plus $x$.

**Example**: 2, 5, 8, 11.

$2 + 3 = 5$; $5 + 3 = 8$… etc.

$x = 3$.

## Fundamental Counting Principle

(The number of possibilities of an event happening) * (the number of possibilities of another event happening) = the total number of possibilities.

**Example**: If you take a multiple choice test with 5 questions, with 4 answer choices for each question, how many test result possibilities are there?

**Solution**: Question 1 has 4 choices; question 2 has 4 choices; etc.

4 * 4 * 4 * 4 * 4 (one for each question) = **1024 possible test results**.

**Linear Systems**

There are two different methods can be used to solve multiple equation linear systems:

- **Substitution method**: This solves for one variable in one equation and substitutes it into the other equation.

    **Example**: Solve: $3y - 4 + x = 0$ and $5x + 6y = 11$.

    1. Step 1: Solve for one variable:
       $3y - 4 = 0$.
       $3y + x = 4$.
       $x = 4 - 3y$.

    2. Step 2: Substitute into the second equation and solve:
       $5(4 - 3y) + 6y = 11$.
       $20 - 15y + 6y = 11$.
       $20 - 9y = 11$.
       $-9y = -9$.
       $y = 1$.

    3. Step 3: Substitute into the first equation:
       $3(1) - 4 + x = 0$.
       $-1 + x = 0$.
       $x = 1$.

       Solution: $x = 1$, $y = 1$.

- **Addition method**: Manipulate one of the equations so that when it is added to the other, one variable is eliminated.

    **Example**: Solve: $2x + 4y = 8$ and $4x + 2y = 10$.

    1. Step 1: Manipulate one equation to eliminate a variable when added together:
       $-2(2x + 4y = 8)$.
       $-4x - 8y = -16$.
       $(-4x - 8y = -16) + (4x + 2y = 10)$.
       $-6y = -6$.
       $y = 1$.

    2. Step 2: Plug into an equation to solve for the other variable:
       $2x + 4(1) = 8$.
       $2x + 4 = 8$.
       $2x = 4$.
       $x = 2$.

       Solution: $x = 2$, $y = 1$.

56

# Quadratics

**Factoring**: Converting $ax^2 + bx + c$ to factored form. Find two numbers that are factors of $c$ and whose sum is $b$.

    **Example**: Factor: $2x^2 + 12x + 18 = 0$.

1. Step 1: If possible, factor out a common monomial:
   $2(x^2 - 6x + 9)$.

2. Step 2: Find two numbers that are factors of 9 and which equal -6 when added:
   $2(x\quad)(x\quad)$.
       -3  , -3

3. Step 3: Fill in the binomials. Be sure to check your answer signs.
   $2(x - 3)(x - 3)$.

4. Step 4: To solve, set each to equal 0.
   $x - 3 = 0$.
   So, $x = 3$.

**Difference of squares**:

$$a^2 - b^2 = (a + b)(a - b).$$

$$a^2 + 2ab + b^2 = (a + b)(a + b).$$

$$a^2 - 2ab + b^2 = (a - b)(a - b).$$

# Permutations

The number of ways a set number of items can be arranged. Recognized by the use of a factorial (n!), with n being the number of items.

If n = 3, then 3! = 3 * 2 * 1 = 6. If you need to arrange n number of things but $x$ number are alike, then n! is divided by $x$!

    **Example**: How many different ways can the letters in the word **balance** be arranged?

    **Solution**: There are 7 letters so $n! = 7!$ and 2 letters are the same so $x! = 2!$ Set up the equation:

$$\frac{7 * 6 * 5 * 4 * 3 * 2 * 1}{2 * 1} = \textbf{2540 ways.}$$

## Combinations

To calculate total number of possible combinations use the formula:

n!/r! (n-r)!   n = # of objects   r = # of objects selected at a time

**Example**: If seven people are selected in groups of three, how many different combinations are possible?

**Solution**:

$$\frac{7*6*5*4*3*2*1}{(3*2*1)(7-3)} = \textbf{210 possible combinations.}$$

## Geometry

- **Acute Angle**: Measures less than $90^o$.

- **Acute Triangle**: Each angle measures less than $90^o$.

- **Obtuse Angle**: Measures greater than $90^o$.

- **Obtuse Triangle**: One angle measures greater than $90^o$.

- **Adjacent Angles**: Share a side and a vertex.

- **Complementary Angles**: Adjacent angles that sum to $90^o$.

- **Supplementary Angles**: Adjacent angles that sum to $180^o$.

- **Vertical Angles**: Angles that are opposite of each other. They are always congruent (equal in measure).

- **Equilateral Triangle**: All angles are equal.

- **Isosceles Triangle**: Two sides and two angles are equal.

- **Scalene**: No equal angles.

- **Parallel Lines**: Lines that will never intersect. Y ‖ X means line Y is parallel to line X.

- **Perpendicular lines**: Lines that intersect or cross to form $90^o$ angles.

- **Transversal Line**: A line that crosses parallel lines.

- **Bisector**: Any line that cuts a line segment, angle, or polygon exactly in half.
- **Polygon**: Any enclosed plane shape with three or more connecting sides (ex. a triangle).

- **Regular Polygon**: Has all equal sides and equal angles (ex. square).

- **Arc**: A portion of a circle's edge.

- **Chord**: A line segment that connects two different points on a circle.

- **Tangent**: Something that touches a circle at only one point without crossing through it.

- **Sum of Angles**: The sum of angles of a polygon can be calculated using $(n-1)180^o$, when $n$ = the number of sides.

## Regular Polygons

Polygon Angle Principle: $S$ = The sum of interior angles of a polygon with $n$-sides.

$S = (n - 2)180$.

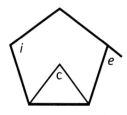

The measure of each central angle ($c$) is $360°/n$.
The measure of each interior angle ($i$) is $(n - 2)180°/n$.
The measure of each exterior angle ($e$) is $360°/n$.

To compare areas of similar polygons: $A_1/A_2 = (\text{side}_1/\text{side}_2)^2$.

## Triangles

The angles in a triangle add up to $180°$.

Area of a triangle = $\frac{1}{2} * b * h$, or $\frac{1}{2}bh$.

Pythagoras' Theorem: $a^2 + b^2 = c^2$.

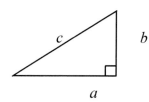

## Trapezoids

Four-sided polygon, in which the bases (and only the bases) are parallel.
Isosceles Trapezoid – base angles are congruent.

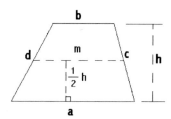

### Area and Perimeter of a Trapezoid

$$m = \frac{1}{2}(a + b)$$

$$Area = \frac{1}{2}h * (a + b) = m * h$$

$$Perimeter = a + b + c + d = 2m + c + d$$

If $m$ is the median then: $m \parallel \overline{AB}$ and $m \parallel \overline{CD}$

59

## Rhombus

Four-sided polygon, in which all four sides are congruent and opposite sides are parallel.

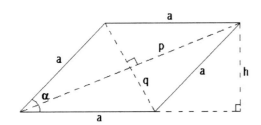

### Area and Perimeter of a Rhombus

$$Perimeter = 4a$$

$$Area = a^2 \sin \alpha = a * h = \frac{1}{2}pq$$

$$4a^2 = p^2 + q^2$$

## Rectangle

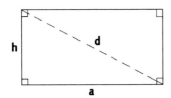

### Area and Perimeter of a Rectangle

$$d = \sqrt{a^2 + h^2}$$

$$a = \sqrt{d^2 - h^2}$$

$$h = \sqrt{d^2 - a^2}$$

$$Perimeter = 2a + 2h$$

$$Area = a \cdot h$$

## Square

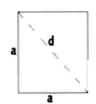

### Area and Perimeter of a Square

$$d = a\sqrt{2}$$

$$Perimeter = 4a = 2d\sqrt{2}$$

$$Area = a^2 = \frac{1}{2}d^2$$

## Circle

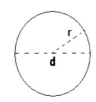

### Area and Perimeter of a Circle

$$d = 2r$$

$$Perimeter = 2\pi r = \pi d$$

$$Area = \pi r^2$$

## Cube

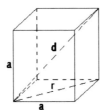

### Area and Volume of a Cube

$$r = a\sqrt{2}$$

$$d = a\sqrt{3}$$

$$Area = 6a^2$$

$$Volume = a^3$$

# Test Your Knowledge: Mathematics

## ORDER OF OPERATIONS

1. $3 * (2 * 4^3) \div 4 = ?$

2. $(4^3 + 2 - 1) = ?$

3. $(5 * 3) * 1 + 5 = ?$

4. $(7^2 - 2^3 - 6) = ?$

5. $(5^3 + 7) * 2 = ?$

## ALGEBRA

6. If Lynn can type a page in $p$ minutes, how many pages can she do in 5 minutes?
   a) $5/p$.
   b) $p - 5$.
   c) $p + 5$.
   d) $p/5$.
   e) $1 - p + 5$.

7. If Sally can paint a house in 4 hours, and John can paint the same house in 6 hours, then how long will it take for both of them to paint the house together?
   a) 2 hours and 24 minutes.
   b) 3 hours and 12 minutes.
   c) 3 hours and 44 minutes.
   d) 4 hours and 10 minutes.
   e) 4 hours and 33 minutes.

8. The sales price of a car is $12,590, which is 20% off the original price. What is the original price?
   a) $14,310.40.
   b) $14,990.90.
   c) $15,290.70.
   d) $15,737.50.
   e) $16,935.80.

9. Solve the following equation for $a$: $2a \div 3 = 8 + 4a$.
   a) -2.4.
   b) 2.4.
   c) 1.3.
   d) -1.3.
   e) 0.

**10.** If $y = 3$, then what is $y^3(y^3 - y)$?

    a) 300.
    b) 459.
    c) 648.
    d) 999.
    e) 1099.

## ALGEBRA 2

**11.** The average of three numbers is $v$. If one of the numbers is $z$ and another is $y$, then what is the remaining number?

    a) $ZY - V.$
    b) $Z/V - 3 - Y.$
    c) $Z/3 - V - Y.$
    d) $3V - Z - Y.$
    e) $V - Z - Y.$

**12.** Mary is reviewing her algebra quiz. She has determined that one of her solutions is incorrect. Which one is it?

    a) $2x + 5(x - 1) = 9; x = 2.$
    b) $p - 3(p - 5) = 10; p = 2.5.$
    c) $4y + 3y = 28; y = 4.$
    d) $5w + 6w - 3w = 64; w = 8.$
    e) $t - 2t - 3t = 32; t = 8.$

**13.** What simple interest rate will Susan need to secure in order to make $2,500 in interest on a $10,000 principal over 5 years?

    a) 4%.
    b) 5%.
    c) 6%.
    d) 7%.
    e) 8%.

**14.** Which of the following is not a rational number?

    a) -4.
    b) 1/5.
    c) 0.8333333...
    d) 0.45.
    e) $\sqrt{2}$.

**AVERAGES and ROUNDING**

**15.** Round 907.457 to the nearest tens place.
   a) 908.0.
   b) 910.
   c) 907.5.
   d) 900.
   e) 907.46.

**16.** What is 1230.932567 rounded to the nearest hundredths place?
   a) 1200.
   b) 1230.9326.
   c) 1230.93.
   d) 1230.
   e) 1230.933.

**17.** Combine the following numbers and round to the nearest tenths place:

   134.679
   -45.548
   -67.8807

   a) 21.3.
   b) 21.25.
   c) -58.97.
   d) -59.0.
   e) 1.

**18.** What is the absolute value of – 9?
   a) -9.
   b) 9.
   c) 0.
   d) -1.
   e) 1.

**19.** What is the median of the following list of numbers: 4, 5, 7, 9, 10, and 12?
   a) 6.
   b) 7.5.
   c) 7.8.
   d) 8.
   e) 9.

**20.** What is the mathematical average of the number of weeks in a year, seasons in a year, and the number of days in January?

 a) 36.
 b) 33.
 c) 32.
 d) 31.
 e) 29.

## BASIC OPERATIONS

**21.** Add $0.98 + 45.102 + 32.3333 + 31 + 0.00009$.

 a) 368.573.
 b) 210.536299.
 c) 109.41539.
 d) 99.9975.
 e) 80.8769543.

**22.** Find $0.12 \div 1$.

 a) 12.
 b) 1.2.
 c) .12.
 d) .012.
 e) .0012.

**23.** $(9 \div 3) * (8 \div 4)$ equals:

 a) 1.
 b) 6.
 c) 72.
 d) 576.
 e) 752.

**24.** $6 * 0 * 5$ equals:

 a) 30.
 b) 11.
 c) 25.
 d) 0.
 e) 27.

**25.** $7.95 \div 1.5$ equals:

 a) 2.4.
 b) 5.3.
 c) 6.2.
 d) 7.3.
 e) 7.5.

**ESTIMATION SEQUENCE**

26. Describe the following sequence in mathematical terms: 144, 72, 36, 18, and 9.
   a) Descending arithmetic sequence.
   b) Ascending arithmetic sequence.
   c) Descending geometric sequence.
   d) Ascending geometric sequence.
   e) Miscellaneous sequence.

27. Which of the following is not a whole number followed by its square?
   a) 1, 1.
   b) 6, 36.
   c) 8, 64.
   d) 10, 100.
   e) 11, 144.

28. There are 12 more apples than oranges in a basket of 36 apples and oranges. How many apples are in the basket?
   a) 12.
   b) 15.
   c) 24.
   d) 28.
   e) 36.

29. Which of the following correctly identifies 4 consecutive odd integers, where the sum of the middle two integers is equal to 24?
   a) 5, 7, 9, 11.
   b) 7, 9, 11, 13.
   c) 9, 11, 13, 15.
   d) 11, 13, 15, 17.
   e) 13, 15, 17, 19.

30. What is the next number in the sequence? 6, 12, 24, 48, ___.
   a) 72.
   b) 96.
   c) 108.
   d) 112.
   e) 124.

## MEASUREMENT PRACTICE

**31.** If the perimeter of a rectangular house is 44 yards, and the length is 36 feet, what is the width of the house?
   a)  30 feet.
   b)  18 yards.
   c)  28 feet.
   d)  32 feet.
   e)  36 yards.

**32.** What is the volume of a cylinder with a diameter of 1 foot and a height of 14 inches?
   a)  2104.91cubic inches.
   b)  1584 cubic inches.
   c)  528 cubic inches.
   d)  904.32 cubic inches.
   e)  264 cubic inches.

**33.** What is the volume of a cube whose width is 5 inches?
   a)  15 cubic inches.
   b)  25 cubic inches.
   c)  64 cubic inches.
   d)  100 cubic inches.
   e)  125 cubic inches.

**34.** A can's diameter is 3 inches, and its height is 8 inches. What is the volume of the can?
   a)  50.30 cubic inches.
   b)  56.57 cubic inches.
   c)  75.68 cubic inches.
   d)  113.04 cubic inches.
   e)  226.08 cubic inches.

**35.** If the area of a square flowerbed is 16 square feet, then how many feet is the perimeter of the flowerbed?
   a)  4.
   b)  12.
   c)  16.
   d)  20.
   e)  24.

## PERCENT and RATIO

**36.** If a discount of 25% off the retail price of a desk saves Mark $45, what was the original price of the desk?

    a) $135.
    b) $160.
    c) $180.
    d) $210.
    e) $215.

**37.** A customer pays $1,100 in state taxes on a newly-purchased car. What is the value of the car if state taxes are 8.9% of the value?

    a) $9.765.45.
    b) $10,876.90.
    c) $12,359.55.
    d) $14,345.48.
    e) $15,745.45.

**38.** How many years does Steven need to invest his $3,000 at 7% to earn $210 in simple interest?

    a) 1 year.
    b) 2 years.
    c) 3 years.
    d) 4 years.
    e) 5 years.

**39.** 35% of what number is 70?

    a) 100.
    b) 110.
    c) 150.
    d) 175.
    e) 200.

**40.** What number is 5% of 2000?

    a) 50.
    b) 100.
    c) 150.
    d) 200.
    e) 250.

## MATHEMATICS PRACTICE

**41.** How long will Lucy have to wait before for her $2,500 invested at 6% earns $600 in simple interest?

    a) 2 years.
    b) 3 years.
    c) 4 years.
    d) 5 years.
    e) 6 years.

**42.** If $r = 5z$ and $15z = 3y$, then $r$ equals:
- a) $y$.
- b) $2y$.
- c) $5y$.
- d) $10y$.
- e) $15y$.

**43.** What is 35% of a number if 12 is 15% of a number?
- a) 5.
- b) 12.
- c) 28.
- d) 33.
- e) 62.

**44.** A computer is on sale for $1,600, which is a 20% discount off the regular price. What is the regular price?
- a) $1800.
- b) $1900.
- c) $2000.
- d) $2100.
- e) $2200.

**45.** A car dealer sells an SUV for $39,000, which represents a 25% profit over the cost. What was the cost of the SUV to the dealer?
- a) $29,250.
- b) $31,200.
- c) $32,500.
- d) $33,800.
- e) $33,999.

**46.** Employees of a discount appliance store receive an additional 20% off of the lowest price on an item. If an employee purchases a dishwasher during a 15% off sale, how much will he pay if the dishwasher originally cost $450?
- a) $280.90.
- b) $287.
- c) $292.50.
- d) $306.
- e) $333.89.

**47.** The city council has decided to add a 0.3% tax on motel and hotel rooms. If a traveler spends the night in a motel room that costs $55 before taxes, how much will the city receive in taxes from him?
- a) 10 cents.
- b) 11 cents.
- c) 15 cents.
- d) 17 cents.
- e) 21 cents.

**48.** Grace has 16 jellybeans in her pocket. She has 8 red ones, 4 green ones, and 4 blue ones. What is the minimum number of jellybeans she must take out of her pocket to ensure that she has one of each color?

    a) 4.
    b) 8.
    c) 12.
    d) 13.
    e) 16.

**49.** You need to purchase a textbook for nursing school. The book costs $80.00, and the sales tax is 8.25%. You have $100. How much change will you receive back?

    a) $5.20.
    b) $7.35.
    c) $13.40.
    d) $19.95.
    e) $21.25.

**50.** Your supervisor instructs you to purchase 240 pens and 6 staplers for the nurse's station. Pens are purchased in sets of 6 for $2.35 per pack. Staplers are sold in sets of 2 for $12.95. How much will purchasing these products cost?

    a) $132.85.
    b) $145.75.
    c) $162.90.
    d) $225.25.
    e) $226.75.

**51.** Two cyclists start biking from a trailhead at different speeds and times. The second cyclist travels at 10 miles per hour and starts 3 hours after the first cyclist, who is traveling at 6 miles per hour. Once the second cyclist starts biking, how much time will pass before he catches up with the first cyclist?

    a) 2 hours.
    b) 4 ½ hours.
    c) 5 ¾ hours.
    d) 6 hours.
    e) 7 ½ hours.

**52.** Jim can fill a pool with water by the bucket-full in 30 minutes. Sue can do the same job in 45 minutes. Tony can do the same job in 1 ½ hours. How quickly can all three fill the pool together?

    a) 12 minutes.
    b) 15 minutes.
    c) 21 minutes.
    d) 23 minutes.
    e) 28 minutes.

53. A study reported that, in a random sampling of 100 women over the age of 35, 8 of the women had been married 2 or more times. Based on the study results, how many women over the age of 35 in a group of 5,000 would likely have been married 2 or more times?
    a) 55.
    b) 150.
    c) 200.
    d) 400.
    e) 600.

54. John is traveling to a meeting that is 28 miles away. He needs to be there in 30 minutes. How fast does he need to go in order to make it to the meeting on time?
    a) 25 mph.
    b) 37 mph.
    c) 41 mph.
    d) 49 mph.
    e) 56 mph.

55. If Steven can mix 20 drinks in 5 minutes, Sue can mix 20 drinks in 10 minutes, and Jack can mix 20 drinks in 15 minutes, then how much time will it take all 3 of them working together to mix the 20 drinks?
    a) 2 minutes and 44 seconds.
    b) 2 minutes and 58 seconds.
    c) 3 minutes and 10 seconds.
    d) 3 minutes and 26 seconds.
    e) 4 minutes and 15 seconds.

56. Jim's belt broke, and his pants are falling down. He has 5 pieces of string. He needs to choose the piece that will be able to go around his 36-inch waist. The piece must be at least 4 inches longer than his waist so that he can tie a knot in it, but it cannot be more that 6 inches longer so that the ends will not show from under his shirt. Which of the following pieces of string will work the best?
    a) 3 feet.
    b) 3 ¾ feet.
    c) 3 ½ feet.
    d) 3 ¼ feet.
    e) 2 ½ feet.

57. In the final week of January, a car dealership sold 12 cars. A new sales promotion came out the first week of February, and the dealership sold 19 cars that week. What was the percent increase in sales from the last week of January compared to the first week of February?
    a) 58%.
    b) 119%.
    c) 158%.
    d) 175%.
    e) 200%.

**58.** If two planes leave the same airport at 1:00 PM, how many miles apart will they be at 3:00 PM if one travels directly north at 150 mph and the other travels directly west at 200 mph?

   a) 50 miles.
   b) 100 miles.
   c) 500 miles.
   d) 700 miles.
   e) 1,000 miles.

**59.** During a 5-day festival, the number of visitors tripled each day. If the festival opened on a Thursday with 345 visitors, what was the attendance on that Sunday?

   a) 345.
   b) 1,035.
   c) 1,725.
   d) 3,105.
   e) 9,315.

**60.** What will it cost to carpet a room with indoor/outdoor carpet if the room is 10 feet wide and 12 feet long? The carpet costs $12.51 per square yard.

   a) $166.80.
   b) $175.90.
   c) $184.30.
   d) $189.90.
   e) $192.20.

**61.** Sally has three pieces of material. The first piece is 1 yard, 2 feet, and 6 inches long; the second piece is 2 yard, 1 foot, and 5 inches long; and the third piece is 4 yards, 2 feet, and 8 inches long. How much material does Sally have?

   a) 7 yards, 1 foot, and 8 inches.
   b) 8 yards, 4 feet, and 4 inches.
   c) 8 yards and 11 inches.
   d) 9 yards and 7 inches.
   e) 10 yards.

**62.** A vitamin's expiration date has passed. It was supposed to contain 500 mg of Calcium, but it has lost 325 mg of Calcium. How many mg of Calcium are left?

   a) 135 mg.
   b) 175 mg.
   c) 185 mg.
   d) 200 mg.
   e) 220 mg.

63. You have orders to give a patient 20 mg of a certain medication. The medication is stored as 4 mg per 5-mL dose. How many milliliters will need to be given?
    a) 15 mL.
    b) 20 mL.
    c) 25 mL.
    d) 30 mL.
    e) 35 mL.

64. You need a 1680 ft$^3$ aquarium, exactly, for your fish. The pet store has four choices of aquariums. The length, width, and height are listed on the box, but not the volume. Which of the following aquariums would fit your needs?
    a) 12 ft, by 12 ft, by 12 ft.
    b) 13 ft, by 15 ft, by 16 ft.
    c) 14 ft, by 20 ft, by 6 ft.
    d) 15 ft, by 16 ft, by 12 ft.
    e) 15 ft, by 12 ft, by 12 ft.

65. Sabrina's boss states that she will increase Sabrina's salary from $12,000 to $14,000 per year if Sabrina enrolls in business courses at a local community college. What percent increase in salary will result from Sabrina taking the business courses?
    a) 15%.
    b) 16.7%.
    c) 17.2%.
    d) 85%.
    e) 117%.

66. Jim works for $15.50 per hour at a health care facility. He is supposed to get a $0.75 per hour raise after one year of service. What will be his percent increase in hourly pay?
    a) 2.7%.
    b) 3.3%.
    c) 133%.
    d) 4.8%.
    e) 105%.

67. Edmond has to sell his BMW. He bought the car for $49,000, but sold it at 20% less. At what price did Edmond sell the car?
    a) $24,200.
    b) $28,900.
    c) $35,600.
    d) $37,300.
    e) $39,200.

**68.** At a company fish fry, half of those in attendance are employees. Employees' spouses make up a third of the attendance. What is the percentage of the people in attendance who are neither employees nor employees' spouses?
- a) 10.5%.
- b) 16.7%.
- c) 25%.
- d) 32.3%.
- e) 38%.

**69.** If Sam can do a job in 4 days that Lisa can do in 6 days and Tom can do in 2 days, how long would the job take if Sam, Lisa, and Tom worked together to complete it?
- a) 0.8 days.
- b) 1.09 days.
- c) 1.23 days.
- d) 1.65 days.
- e) 1.97 days.

**70.** Sarah needs to make a cake and some cookies. The cake requires 3/8 cup of sugar, and the cookies require 3/5 cup of sugar. Sarah has 15/16 cups of sugar. Does she have enough sugar, or how much more does she need?
- a) She has enough sugar.
- b) She needs 1/8 of a cup of sugar.
- c) She needs 3/80 of a cup of sugar.
- d) She needs 4/19 of a cup of sugar.
- e) She needs 1/9 of a cup of sugar.

# Test Your Knowledge: Mathematics – Answers

1. 96.

2. 65.

3. 20.

4. 35.

5. 264.

6. a).

7. a).

8. d).

9. a).

10. c).

11. d).

12. e).

13. b).

14. e).

15. b).

16. c).

17. a).

18. b).

19. d).

20. e).

21. c).

22. c).

23. b).

24. d).

25. b).

26. c).

27. e).

28. c).

29. c).

30. b).

31. a).

32. b).

33. e).

34. b).

35. c).

36. c).

37. c).

38. a).

39. e).

40. b).

41. c).

42. a).

43. c).

44. c).

45. b).

46. d).

47. d).

48. d).

49. c).

50. a).

51. b).

52. d).

53. d).

54. e).

55. b).

56. d).

57. a).

58. c).

59. e).

60. a).

61. d).

62. b).

63. c).

64. c).

65. b).

66. d).

67. e).

68. b).

69. b).

70. a).

# **Final Thoughts**

In the end, we know that you will be successful in taking the TABE. Although the road ahead may at times be challenging, if you continue your hard work and dedication (just like you are doing to prepare right now!), you will find that your efforts will pay off.

If you are struggling after reading this book and following our guidelines, we sincerely hope that you will take note of our advice and seek additional help. Start by asking friends about the resources that they are using. If you are still not reaching the score you want, consider getting the help of a TABE tutor.

If you are on a budget and cannot afford a private tutoring service, there are plenty of independent tutors, including college students who are proficient in TABE subjects. You don't have to spend thousands of dollars to afford a good tutor or review course.

We wish you the best of luck and happy studying. Most importantly, we hope you enjoy your coming years – after all, you put a lot of work into getting there in the first place.

Sincerely,
The Trivium Team

CPSIA information can be obtained at www.ICGtesting.com
Printed in the USA
LVOW09s2201100414

381270LV00009B/136/P